Introduction
My Story

'One day you will tell your story of how you overcame what you went through and it will be someone else's survival guide.' – Brené Brown

'I've rented a flat, down the road,' I tell my husband in a tone that makes it clear I expect him to be impressed with my organisational skills.

He looks at me blankly.

'So that we can "bird's nest", you know?'

He clearly doesn't know.

I continue: 'That way, the kids stay here, and we move in and out depending on who's with the kids that week.'

I'm met with silence.

What doesn't he get? I've just told him we are separating, but that it's going to be okay because I have worked it all out. A friend of ours has a flat she only uses once a week, just down the road, and has said we can rent it for a three-month trial while we find our feet in our separation.

'What do you think?' I ask.

Unsurprisingly, Jimmy, my husband, doesn't think much of

my idea. Nor is he willing to credit me for my exceptional organisational skills in light of the fact that, in his eyes, I have just flippantly blown up our life as he knew it. He's still stuck on the 'we're separating' part. I'm baffled because it's clear we've been unhappy for ages, and I can't believe this has come as a surprise to him. But, apparently, it has, and so we sit in silence on the sofa for a few moments before he says, simply, 'What the actual fuck?'

The ensuing conversation is a mixture of going over *really* old, well-trodden ground and brand-new information. It's probably the first time in our relationship that we've been unapologetically honest about how we're feeling. I've just told him I want to separate – what have we got to lose? I tell him how I hate everything about him but that I can't quite put my finger on why. I tell him that every time he walks into a room, I want to walk out because I'm afraid that if I stay I'll punch him or stab him, and I tell him that everything he does irritates me. He tells me that I'm impossible to live with, that I'm always angry, and that he has *no idea* what he can do about it. I throw my head back, exasperated, and tell him that it's not fucking *rocket science*: 'Be on my fucking team!' I scream.

This conversation is a lot like a million other conversations we've had over the years, but something does feel different. This isn't a fight born from one too many dirty plates left on the counter above the dishwasher. This isn't the inevitable emotional earthquake after several tense tremors that manifest as door slamming, a series of 'I'm fines', and the silent treatment. This is an actual conversation where we're not deflecting. We're not skirting around the

The Mental Load Diaries

The Mental Load Diaries

How I learned to juggle life, love and the neverending to-do list.

Cat Sims

GALLERY BOOKS UK

Simon & Schuster UK Ltd
1st Floor
222 Gray's Inn Road
London WC1X 8HB

A CIP catalogue record for this book is available from the British Library

Hardback ISBN: 978-1-3985-4940-1
eBook ISBN: 978-1-3985-4941-8

Typeset in Bembo Std by
Palimpsest Book Production Limited, Falkirk, Stirlingshire

Printed and Bound in the UK
using 100% Renewable Electricity at CPI Group (UK) Ltd

MIX
Paper | Supporting
responsible forestry
FSC® C013604

Contents

Introduction: My Story   vii

1: The Privilege of the Mental Load   1

2: The Generational Hand-Me-Downs   13

3: He Had Three Nipples and a Shoulder   29
   He Could Dislocate

4: The Rom-Con   41

5: Girl on Tour   52

6: Splashdown   63

7: Bringing Home the Bacon (and Cooking it Too)   74

8: The Disney Dad and the Evil (Step)Mum   84

9: Keeping My Side of the Street Clean   94

10: The Sock that Broke the Camel's Back   101

11: Addicted To . . . Everything   111

12: Burn, Baby Burn   127

13: Apparently, Couples' Therapy Isn't a Competition   137

14: I'm the Problem, It's Me   155

15: Hormoaning   162

16: The Shit-Sandwich Generation   172

17: Handling Your Balls   182

18: The Self-Care Ball   188

19: If Weaponised Incompetence Were a Person, it Would Be a Kid   200

20: Doing it for the 'Gram   209

21: The Men-tal Load   218

22: Nurture *Not* Nature   232

23: Becoming Bilingual   243

24: When the Exception Proves the Rule   250

25: Final Thoughts   253

Epilogue: The Mental Load List that Went Viral   259

Endnotes   263

Acknowledgements   265

real issues of deep-seated resentment and pain by making it all about the left-up loo seat or the unmade bed. By sitting Jimmy down to tell him I want to separate, I have inadvertently made space, for the first time, for a conversation about how we are really feeling beneath the anger ignited by the daily microaggressions that come when you decide to entangle your life with another human being's. It's uncharted territory for us after eight years of being in a relationship. It's messy and painful and exhausting, but it finally makes clear to both of us what I knew to be true: we are not happily married, and we need to either shit, or get off the pot.

It's because I can feel that this conversation is different that I agree, reluctantly, to go back to couples' therapy. We've been down this road before, and while I don't hold any hope that it'll be any more useful than the last time, I do want to be able to look my kids in the eye and tell them that, even though Mummy and Daddy aren't together anymore, we did *everything* we could to try to make it work. If I refuse to go to couples' therapy, I won't be able to do that, and I can't bear to be the villain in this story. I don't want *anyone* to be the villain – I may not want to be married to Jimmy anymore at this moment, but I also know that I love him deeply and, if all things were perfect, he's the one I'd want it to work out with. It's just a shame that isn't the way it's going to be.

I call my friend and tell her the flat rental is on hold, but that I'll be back in touch shortly. Jimmy calls our therapist and books us in for the next day, and so begins our journey back to marital harmony. For the next six weeks we don't dare to speak outside of the therapist's office. We make nice in front of the kids but as soon as they are out of sight, we bounce away from each other like magnets repelling. As the truth bombs drop relentlessly in therapy, we begin to understand that, if we have a chance of surviving, we cannot hold back. We have to say all the things we think and feel, and we just have to hope that we can both hang on to our deep-seated desire to make it work.

Therapy gives us the space to say the first thing that comes into our heads, our reactive responses, but it also gives us the time and space to explore what's *really* pissing us off, or hurting us, or making us feel unheard, abandoned, jealous, insecure. I learn that the fatal flaw in our relationship is this: neither of us feel *kept in mind*. I'm flabbergasted to learn that it refers to him as well as to me.

'But I do *everything* for him,' I complain. 'I cook his food, I clean his pants and the shit stains he leaves in the toilet bowl. I birth children, I research all the stuff, I buy all the stuff, I plan all the stuff. I make sure his mum gets a birthday present, I make Christmas magical, I change the beds and vacuum and make sure the kids' lunches are paid for, and what does he do? I don't know how he has the *nerve* to suggest that I don't keep him in mind. I'm exhausted from keeping him and everyone else in mind. It's all I fucking do!' I shout.

That was the root of my resentment: The Mental Load, the invisible labour, the unpaid work I do, all in the name of love for my family. The therapist named it, and I cried with relief. I began to understand that I had become consumed by the spiteful belief that I do everything for everyone and no one ever took a moment to recognise it or appreciate it. It had, I realised, infected every interaction I had with my husband

and my family. They just didn't get it. Is it even possible that they ever would?

I was also beginning to realise, as I heard my husband tell his story, that it had made me blind to his resentments, to his feelings. He felt like living with me was impossible. I was a perfectionist, nothing was ever good enough, he felt constantly battered by criticism, eye-rolls and a tsunami of dissatisfaction. He wondered whether I even liked him, let alone loved him. He knew he wasn't a bad guy but he didn't know how to be a good enough guy.

Fuck, I thought, *this isn't a small thing*, and I was right. It took two years of weekly therapy and hard emotional graft for us to get to a point where we weren't seething with unrecognised resentments and anger, and even longer for us to figure out how to manage those resentments, when they popped up, without wanting to rip each other's heads off and shit down their throat.

Honestly, as I write this, we're still figuring all of that out, but there's one thing I do know for sure: *the mental load that existed, unnamed, between us was a virus that destroyed us, silently, from the inside out.* But in some ways that was just the most obvious symptom of a much bigger problem. The fuel on the burning embers of our resentments was our total inability to communicate with each other. It was as if we were in a constant state of fight or flight, always on high alert, just waiting for the other to say something that we could construe as critical. When that happened, all bets were off. Let the screaming begin.

Therapy was our marital sat-nav. It revealed short cuts that allowed us to get from problem to solution without taking the scenic route through Shit-Loss City, Resentment Ridge and Silent-Treatment-On-Sea. Like a sat-nav, though, it couldn't do the driving for us. We had to do that. We could have gone to therapy, been given directions and stayed exactly where we were. Or, we could have just continued driving with no direction. Either option would have taken us to the dead-end of divorce. Fortunately, we listened to the instructions we were given and both did our part to make sure we got to where we needed to be, which, if it wasn't Marital Bliss Beach, was something close, like Generally Peaceful Plaza.

This book is my attempt to unravel the mystery of the insidious beast that we now know as the mental load and how it has inadvertently affected my sense of self and my relationships my whole life. Where did it come from? Why are women burdened by it? Can it ever be evenly distributed? Can a marriage or a relationship survive the mental load? What do we need to do to break the cycle?

I can't promise you any magical solutions to this age-old problem. I'm not a therapist, or a sociologist, or an expert in gender politics. I'm a white woman, in my forties, married with two children – a walking stereotype. None of my problems are unique or special, and this isn't a book designed to 'fix' the mental load, or even to raise awareness around it. Nor is it going to fix your marriage (probably).

I'm no expert on, well, anything really. What I *am* is a writer, and so it's *that* skill that I bring, to tell my own story about how the mental load affected (and, in some ways, continues to affect) my mental health, my relationships, my career, my sense of self, my family. There are some very clever and knowledgeable people who have written loads of other books that are designed to actually help you. This isn't one of those books. This is just a book documenting my own experience and, in doing so, I hope it will spark connectivity among the women and men who read it.

And yes, I did say *men*, because this is not a book written solely for women. It's a book written for people in relationships to help them navigate this invisible emotional pandemic that I truly believe is responsible for the death of so many relationships. It's a book that I hope will make you laugh and cry in equal measure. It's a book that, at times, gets a bit sweary. It's not a book full of statistics and teaching points. Essentially, it's a story book for the adults of this world designed to make you − yes, *you* − feel like you're not on your own, and in turn, to do the same thing for me.

I don't want this book to be the silenced gun in your own relationship. I never want this to be a book that women use to beat their partners with. I don't want it to be the kind of book that is left out, passive-aggressively, on their partner's bedside table, tabbed and highlighted extensively in order to try to make a point. I want it to be a book that you read, that incites honest and vulnerable conversation between you and your partner, you and your friends, you and your parents. I hope it's a book that gives you the confidence to know that it is possible to share the mental load in a way that makes a difference, but to do that, it also needs to be a book that forces you to reflect on your own behaviour and your own part in the dynamic.

So, while this is a book about the mental load and what essentially amounts to the generational persecution of women at the hands of it, it's really a book about how *you* have to change how you manage and react to it. Actually, it's about how *we* have to change how we manage and react to it because, like most things, it's become painfully obvious to me that changing the world isn't the remit of politicians and lawmakers. It's the remit of women, who will do it efficiently, kindly and resolutely without needing to make a fuss about it. When our children are able to grow up in a world where there are no pink and blue jobs, it won't be because powerful, white men stood at lecterns and shouted about what we should and shouldn't do. It'll be because couples like you and your partner quietly started setting an example in your own homes, showing your families, kids and work colleagues how to own their shit and not act like a dick. Because when it comes down to it, that's really what it's all about.

So, in advance of you reading this book, let me say thank you. Thank you for reading it and making me feel less alone in this world that is struggling to find the balance of labour.

Cat

1

The Privilege of the Mental Load

'When we pause to contemplate, all of our problems are
simply our privileges in disguise.' – Dr Salma Farook,
What Your Soul Already Knows

Before we get into it, it's really important that I acknowledge
the fact that not all mental loads are created equal. Yes, it's
relative and yes, everyone's hard is different, but sometimes I
feel as if the more privileged among us (and I include myself
in that) use that to justify a luxurious soak in the puddle of
self-pity. It also makes it easy for those who believe their load
to be harder, tougher and heavier than others to project their
feelings outwards in anger. Wherever you sit on the spectrum
of emotional labour, please know that this all comes from a
place of good intent. It comes from a place of identifying
feelings within my own experience that I know other people
have felt.

The trappings of our mental loads may look very different.
Our houses will be different sizes, our family set-ups will vary,
our support villages may or may not exist and the amounts in
bank accounts and pay cheques will differ. We will all prioritise

different things, whether that's our career, our relationship or our role as parents. But whatever it is that you carry around in your head, on a loop, I am certain there is an inherent feeling for most of us that, as women in this society today, it's easy to feel a resounding lack of support, whether that's on a micro level at home, or on a macro level in the world more generally. Sure, your neighbour may have a nanny and you may be a single mum, but that doesn't mean her load is any less difficult for her.

Let's get the obvious out of the way: I am a white, middle-class woman in a cis-heterosexual relationship with a fairly traditional set-up. We earn good money, we own a house in London, and while we can't afford a cleaner or childcare, we can afford nice clothes, a holiday once a year and extra-curricular activities for the kids. Our house is warm and our fridge is generally full. For that I have nothing but gratitude, but I'd be lying if I *always* had an attitude of gratitude. There are definitely times when I forget how easy my life is, how little friction there is between me waking up in the morning and me getting through to the end of the day.

That doesn't mean to say I move gracefully and blissfully through the world on a daily basis – I absolutely don't. Anyone following me on Instagram will know that I am more than partial to the occasional pity-party, but I have definitely been guilty of *assuming* that everyone consuming my content knows that the whining and the whingeing comes with a heavy side-order of self-awareness. I *do* know how lucky I am, I *do* know that my life is #blessed and I want to make this abso-lutely clear: *I write this book as a product of a society that favours women like me.*

At the risk of sounding like an inspirational quote tile, *everyone's hard is different*, and as long as that's acknowledged, I think we can all come together as women under an unspoken but universally agreed truth that it's not about what someone's life looks like from the outside or what the trappings are; it's about whether we, as women, on an individual level, feel supported and heard by the people closest to us and, if we don't, then that's a pain we can all relate to. *That's* the pain I want to talk about in this book.

So, please know I am hyper-aware of my privilege and the effect that it might have on how the messages in this book are perceived, but I think failing to acknowledge, clearly, that many women would happily swap their mental load for mine would show a real lack of self-awareness. I know that, comparatively, it may not seem as if I have a lot to wang on about. After all, it's easy to scoff and wonder how hard my life can really be with a husband, two kids, a house we own and two incomes (albeit, completely unreliable incomes!). After all, there are single mums, single dads, parents of colour, parents with disabilities, chronic and terminal illnesses, parents in poverty. There are parents whose kids are disabled, or whose partner is sick. Parents who have kids struggling with mental health issues, neurodiversity, addiction, eating disorders . . . you name it. When I think about this, I'm almost embarrassed that it's *me* writing this book and not someone who could *really* write about the hardships of existing in this world. But, I'm not writing this book because my mental load is the worst. It's not a book bragging about how I win at the mental load and how my life is harder than everyone else's. God no! Instead, I am writing this book because, of all the skills I could have been born with, it's my ability to translate the things that make us feel alone and lonely into stories that make us feel less so.

Intersectionality is one of those words that has been thrown around in the last few years, across social media and within conversations about privilege, race, sexuality and a host of other social issues. The *Oxford Dictionary* defines intersectionality as:

The interconnected nature of social categorizations such as race, class, and gender, regarded as creating overlapping and interdependent systems of discrimination or disadvantage; a theoretical approach based on such a premise.

The *Merriam-Webster* definition is:

The complex, cumulative way in which the effects of multiple forms of discrimination (such as racism, sexism, and classism) combine, overlap, or intersect especially in the experiences of marginalized individuals or groups

To put it more practically, I'm a woman who struggles with the mental load and the societal expectations placed upon women when it comes to the domestic sphere. My experience of that has been tough and that experience is valid, but it's not enough to convey my experience as the defining one. Yes, I've been clear about my advantages, but it would be remiss of me not to acknowledge the additional disadvantages that other women are subject to *on top* of the expectations around unpaid and emotional labour.

Not to state the obvious but I am not a woman of colour, I'm not a single mother, I don't have a disability, I don't come from a culture or religion where women's rights are severely infringed upon. I don't come from a low socio-economic background, I'm educated, I'm married to a man who loves me, I have two happy, healthy kids who don't have any additional needs. I have a job and private health insurance. I have a fucking sausage dog. A miniature one. If you're wondering what on earth it *is* that I find difficult about life, don't worry, I get it.

There are women for whom couples' therapy isn't an option. Maybe they're financially excluded from it or maybe there's a cultural shame surrounding therapy in general. Perhaps those women aren't safe to question the domestic status quo with their partners, let alone request that those partners help them with it. I'm aware of these things and while I hope that this book may offer some comfort to those women, I am also painfully aware that any guidance or advice it offers will be useless to someone without the same advantages that I have.

The intersectionality of this privilege is real and very nuanced and I acknowledge clearly that I can only comment on my own experience from my own place in the world. I have no wish or desire to talk for, or on behalf of, anyone else, but please know that I am hyper-aware of my limited experience and therefore conscious that this book will not be for everyone. That being said, if you're a woman in a relationship with someone of the opposite sex, there will be elements of this book that are relatable, comforting and maybe even helpful. If you are a woman in a relationship with another woman, I'm sure there will be a lot of things you identify with, but perhaps not as much. If you are a woman of colour, a woman struggling financially, a single mum, a man, a man in a relationship with another man, a transgender woman or man . . . I don't know how much of this will translate because, quite simply, I don't have your lived experience.

There are also parts of this book for which I have reached out to people for their perspective and feelings. Part of that is down to my own curiosity about this phenomenon that has become known as the mental load and how rigidly that applies to gender or whether it's an inevitable dynamic of any partnership. But part of it is also a keen awareness of my limited experience in this world and a willingness to acknowledge that I only know how the mental load affects me and my family.

Despite all this, rather than focus on the varying amount of privilege among us as women, and use that as a stick to beat each other with, it might also be worth noting the specific disadvantages that we all experience *because* we are women, since the patriarchy's PR job on the mental load has been nothing short of spectacular.

Branding it 'women's work', 'homemaking', 'housekeeping', 'kin keeping' and reducing it where possible to nothing more than cleaning and therefore effectively filing it under 'menial tasks' was a stroke of genius from the misogynistic hive mind. 'Women's work' makes it sound like it's some sort of hobby that they allow us to do. 'Homemaking' implies some sort of creativity or skill and the last time I checked, it doesn't take much skill to clean skiddies off the toilet bowl. 'Housekeeping' sounds a bit more responsible; like something our male partners pay us for, for tax reasons, and doesn't 'kin keeping' sound like the tip of the matriarchal pyramid? Like we're the boss in charge of all the 'kin'?

The irony is that managing the mental load, which is, if we're honest, managing a family and a household, is nothing short of CEO-level shit. I have a friend, who once said that, in the middle of an argument with her partner over the mental load, she said, 'Managing this house and this family is like running a business and, let me tell you, if that was the case, you'd be fired.' I remember laughing uncontrollably, but also feeling relief flood through my body, because she was right. It was the first time I had heard someone acknowledge the gravity of the job we do as women, the level of skill it requires and the energy it takes.

This constant minimising of the mental load has meant that, socially, we all grew up believing that it was just one element of our role as women, that it wasn't that big of a deal, that any woman worth her salt should be more than capable of managing a bit of cleaning. Of course, when it came to it, when we actually found ourselves in charge of the 'house-keeping', we quickly realised cleaning the bogs and doing the laundry was just the tip of the monumental-load iceberg (do you see what I did there?), but in the face of the patriarchal gaslighting around the concept, we started to question ourselves. We started to think that maybe *we* were the problem, because how hard can running a vacuum around a house and making a few beds really be?

In my (very humble) opinion, the historical and supremely insidious marketing campaign done around the mental load by our patriarchal society has been the heaviest and tightest shackle around women's ankles. I fear that, unless every parent on the planet of this generation (and the next two or three) consciously and consistently undermines the idea that 'a woman's work is in the home', we will never emerge from the weight of that edict. How are women ever going to have the same balls-out confidence as men when it comes to demanding our worth in the workplace when, in our homes, our most valuable skill set – the management of a domestic corporation (which, by the way, is a highly transferable skill set) – is exploited every day and largely unacknowledged? Even the most appreciative of partners tend to just see the high-profile results of their woman's work. They may thank you for ironing their shirts, for cooking dinner or for taking care of the kids while they played golf. But, chances are, they don't notice the clean skirting boards, the fact that the kitchen cupboards have been cleared of crumbs to deter mice, or the fourteen times you wiped down the kitchen surfaces that day.

So if we're going to get angry about the privilege involved in a discussion of the mental load, let's not fight among ourselves. Let's not worry about whether or not Sally down the road deserves to complain about the mental load because she's got a cleaner when Doris is a single mum to three kids. The privilege we really need to get pissed off about is that which our male partners have, simply because of what they have between their legs, what they've been trained to believe is their responsibility, and how easily and seamlessly they have been told they can and should move through the world.

There is hope, though – I truly believe that. Yes, there's hope when it comes to men stepping up and recognising the reality of the mental load, but more importantly, there's hope among the female fellowship of the world. I do see change. I see women turning up on social media and saying, 'I get it!' rather than, 'You signed up for this . . . stop complaining.' I see women finding comfort in the common tales we spin on Instagram or TikTok about how we're struggling, how our brains are fried, how we can't remember the words for things, or the names of people we see every day, or why we went into a room because we are so overloaded with the relentless minutiae of managing a household and a family. I truly think I'm seeing less defensiveness among women when it comes to this topic and more virtual hand-holding. It's not all gone – of course – but it's receding, slowly but surely.

When it comes down to it, I wanted to write this book for every single one of you. I want it to speak to the generations of women who have been mentally abused by a system that requires us to manage it from behind the scenes and look pretty at the end of it while we stand next to a man getting credit for it. I want to speak to the women who choose to fall in line with the patriarchy – the 'trad wives' as they're labelled – and I want them to know that if that's what *they* want, then they have my full support, but I also want to ask them not to claim that their version of womanhood is the *right* one, the only acceptable one. Instead, let's acknowledge it as one option among many from which we are all free to choose. I want to speak to those women who broke under the pressure of 'having it all' and were labelled weak-minded, unable to cope or 'sensitive'. I want to speak to every woman who's ever been told, 'You should have asked,' or been asked, 'What have you got to complain about?' I want to be heard by those women who have been kept down by men who 'take care of the big-ticket items' and have been made to feel like managing the mental load alone was, at best, the very least they could do or, at worst, something they should be grateful to have the chance to do.

So, please know, I see my privilege. I am trying my best to write carefully from within it and if occasionally I slip up, then please know it wasn't intentional. I want to be self-aware but I also want to be honest and, sometimes, those two things are a little incompatible. Whatever the trappings of your life, the heavy, heavy feeling of overwhelm, fear, anxiety, pressure and juggling is relatable, and it's this that I want to focus on.

I also want to ask a favour of you. I want to ask you to give me and all other women the grace to find things hard. I want to ask everyone to make space for the reality of all women and to avoid making this into a competition. If there's one thing that I admire the patriarchy for, it's their ability to manipulate women into turning on each other. So many of the social expectations that we try to fulfil as women were created by men – by their expectations, their gaze, their unwillingness to do certain jobs. And at some point, women started climbing over themselves to be recognised in a man's world and along the way we got used to elbowing each other out of the way, tearing each other down, stepping on the faces of women beneath us.

I don't want to exist as part of a machine that operates in that way anymore. I don't want this book to make you angry because my life is easier than yours. Or make you uncomfortable because you have more privilege than I do. Wouldn't it be great if, as women, we could give each other the grace to stand in our own experience, whatever that looks like, without shame? Wouldn't it be novel if we looked at how this book can help us rather than how we can use it to beat each other over the head? Wouldn't it be wonderful if our first thought was at best kindness and at worst indifference – a kind of indifference that just required you to put the book down and move on with your life rather than come up with a million reasons why you're right and I'm wrong. I heard a saying once that pretty much changed my life: *Does it need to be said by me? Does it need to be said now? Does it need to be said at all?* And as I move through the world, I'm starting to realise that, invariably, the answer to all those questions is 'no'.

This book is my attempt to use my power and privilege to speak up, and I encourage you to do the same thing. Where we can, we must use our influence in our own small corners of the world to make the changes that allow for women and men to decide just how they manage the mental load within their own families. I think we're guilty of forgetting that not every woman wants their husbands to take on half of the mental load. Not all women see their role as the managers of the mental load as an unfair burden, not all women want to work *and* have children, not all women, not all women, not all women. And that's okay. It's not our job to impose our opinions about how much we should or shouldn't share the responsibility of the mental load; it's our job as women to make the space for all women to consciously choose what they want *their* role in *their* world to look like regardless of whether that looks the same as ours or not.

I want this to be a book from which you take what you

want and you leave the rest. It's like a buffet. Read it and watch out for the similarities, not the differences. It's going to be a wild read and I'm excited and more than a little nervous to share it with you. But first we must start where all good tales start . . . at the beginning.

2

The Generational Hand-Me-Downs

'Just imagine what a generation of unbroken women could do.'
– Taryn de Vere

My first thought as I write this book is: *Fuck, I've bitten off way more than I can chew*. But, as I've come to learn, the first thought is always a rogue mental directive designed to help me fight my way out of a life-or-death situation, and, as important as I believe this book is, let's be honest, it's not life or death. So, I wait for my second thought, and there it is: *You don't have to define the mental load as a global concept, Cat, you idiot. You just have to tell your version of it.*

And, breathe. That, *that*, I can do.

My mental load was a gift from my mother, and, in turn, it was a gift from her mother. In fact, it's an emotional heirloom that has been handed down through the generations from mother to daughter without question until fairly recently. I saw my mother take on the occasional part-time job, but they always became unmanageable in the face of my father's career, which required him to work away for long periods at a time. I saw a rabid anxiety in her regarding 'the state of the house'. If guests were coming, woe betide you if you did anything in the house that would suggest someone lived there, such as make a cup of tea or use the loo. I saw her become the primary carer for me, the cooker of meals, the shopper of food, the maker of beds, the pusher of vacuums, the ironer of her husband's shirts. It never, *ever* occurred to her, or my father, or me, that this division of labour was perhaps a little unfair. This was, quite simply, the way things were.

And let me tell you, my mum was pissed as hell about it. I'm not sure she could have verbalised it. Outside of academia, the language for what she was feeling, and why, didn't exist, but, boy, were those resentments made clear on a daily basis. She was angry and resentful and did a lot of huffing and puffing and eye-rolling. There were many fights between my mum and dad about why he was always away, and when he was home, why he was at the pub. Numerous dinners were left to incinerate in the oven when my dad had more than 'a quick pint at The Fleece'. Dad would get incandescent about money, or something else quintessentially male in the sphere of life admin. And then there were lots of fights about things that I had no idea about; all I heard was the screaming. Looking back, I can see now that my mum spent that period of her life feeling very 'not kept in mind' and Dad felt like he couldn't do right for doing wrong. Essentially, they too struggled to communicate, and that was my relationship blueprint.

I did what most little girls do. I looked to my mother as the model for my future self. It was hardwired into me by osmosis that when I grew up and got married, I would be responsible for cooking, cleaning, shopping, childcare. That's what women did. But, I was also told by my father that I would make an exceptional lawyer. This was based solely on the debates we used to have in the car on long journeys down to the South of France, during which we would bat arguments between us like a shuttlecock. My mother was present on these journeys, but for some reason, she was never included in the conversation. It didn't occur to me that this was unkind, or that she may have felt left out; it was just assumed that this wasn't her sphere. Sure, we deferred to her when it came to what sandwich we were going to eat, and when we needed to reapply sunscreen, but debates about animal rights or politics? No. That was between my father and me. On the odd occasion when she would interject, neither of us took her seriously.

What other reality could there possibly have been for my mum? She was a woman who had grown up in a working-class mining family in South Yorkshire. A woman who, from the moment she splashed down earthside, had been brought up in a community so traditionally gendered that it was women who were to be seen and not heard. As for the kids – well, it was best if they weren't even seen. It was a strict Catholic upbringing where the expectations regarding the behaviour of girls were much higher than those of their male counterparts and so the restrictions were harsher. There was very little in the way of inspiration or aspiration if you were a girl growing up in a 1950s working-class community, and I remain in awe of my mum, who in many ways was able to defy her fated path and choose a different life, one where she was able to take up more space. Not enough space, but more nonetheless.

For those of us who grew up with Boomer parents, it's inevitable that, despite all our best efforts, we have still unknowingly taken on some old-fashioned ideas about gender. Some of us have been better at overriding these than others – I think on some level I was quite a slow learner. It took longer than it should have done for me to realise I was, subconsciously, holding on to some pretty archaic ideas.

My ideas about what being a 'man' and what being a 'woman' meant, for example, were actually pretty traditional. How could they not be? All I'd seen was traditional tropes play out around me when I was growing up. I just assumed that my husband would earn more than me, that I wouldn't have to bear the responsibility of the family economy, because I'd never seen a version of a marriage where that wasn't the case. I definitely *wanted* to be the kind of woman who was happy to be the main breadwinner, while my supportive partner stayed at home and took care of the house, but there was also part of me that desired the security of being looked after financially by the man I loved.

Symptomatic of that belief was, naturally, that I would take on the responsibility of domestic life. Of course, at the root of this thought process was the fundamental and unde- niable truth that men did, indeed, earn more money than women. No matter a woman's levels of confidence or self- esteem, not many of us who grew up in the 80s and 90s had the balls to suggest that we were going to be the one to challenge that. Our literal lack of balls somehow left us labelled as weak, unable, vulnerable. It didn't occur to us to consider the reality that a man's balls are, in fact, his weak spot, while our vaginas and vulvas are strong enough to house, grow and birth real-life humans. As the meme goes, 'Those things can take a pounding.'

We've also been conditioned to sneer at those women who choose more traditional roles. I'm not here to judge. I'm just suggesting that maybe some of us are guilty of feeling a bit superior when it comes to women who have no interest in glass ceilings or 50/50 childcare, and it's okay to examine whether this is true for you in even the smallest way. Accepting that there was a part of me, no matter how small or subconscious, that negatively judged women who weren't ripping their aprons off and racing out of the kitchen, didn't make me a bad person. It made me an honest person, and if I was ever going to be in with a chance of doing better, I had to be clear on what I was wrong about. What I realised was that any belief or idea I had that pitted one type of woman against another, was probably pretty archaic thinking and should be challenged.

Let's take the school fair as an example.

You're a mum, and you have been bombarded with emails stating that your child needs to come to school with a cake for the bake sale (as if that kind of thing just happens because a letter asked it to be so, with no acknowledgement of the blood, sweat and tears, literally, that will go into making that request a reality).

Mum #1 will be delighted – nay, excited – by the prospect of baking a cake. They may even relish it as a chance to spend some quality time with their child as they bake it together. For this mum, it is truly a responsibility they enjoy and find value in. Cake baking is their lane, their wheelhouse, and they are excited to be able to fulfil a task of motherhood that they will excel in and that will make their children proud.

Then there's Mum #2. She is not a baker. Or a cake maker, or a candlestick maker. She is not crafty in the slightest and does not have the time to bake a cake. The thought of baking with her child brings her out in stress hives, and so she resolves to pop into the supermarket on the way home and buy something. Will she leave it in the packaging or spruce it up so that it looks a bit more like she made it? Who knows . . . she'll see whether she's got time.

Both these women think they are fully secure in their decision and what it says about them as women and mothers, but, let's be honest, that's not true. In reality, whether she fully realises it or not, Mum #1 will almost certainly judge Mum #2 for not being a good mum and Mum #2 will almost certainly judge Mum #1 for being a shit woman. They won't say it out loud – unless they're really mean – but there will be some need deep within themselves to justify their differing choices as women by putting the other woman down.

I could come up with a myriad of examples of how women divide themselves up so that the patriarchy can conquer. Our rational brains know there is no right or wrong way to turn up to a bloody bake sale, but the other part of our brain, the brain that we have very little control over curating, holds on to this irrepressible belief that we are, somehow, always fucking it all up a little bit and that other women, who do things differently, are simply highlighting those fuck-ups, and so we must, in our own minds at least, undermine them and the values they represent.

If I'm honest, I have internally and silently judged women who just wanted to get married, have kids and stay at home – and here's why. I tried it. I tried being a stay-at-home mum back when my first baby was born, and I couldn't do it. I hated every minute of it. I was legitimately pretty bad at it, but not because I was a defective mother or woman; I was bad at it because it was really fucking hard and I had spent my entire life building up a deep-seated resistance to asking for help or admitting I couldn't do things. I'd come to believe early on in my life that if I was to survive this world, I would have to be entirely self-sufficient. The reasons for this I will divulge later, when we know each other a little better, but suffice to say for now, my robust self-reliance, my physical exhaustion and my failing mental health combined to kneecap me as a stay-at-home mum. So, when I see women thriving in that environment, not having to leave their kids at daycare, or not counting down the minutes until they can just be on their own, I make that about me. I internalise that as proof that I am a shit mum and somewhere, somehow, that comes out as judgement. I suppose it's what you'd call textbook projection. I am, as it turns out, human after all.

It's an uncomfortable truth to acknowledge. That some-where, rooted inside us, we haven't quite let go of the idea that there are 'natural' roles that men and women should play in society; that there are ways we should act according to our gender, when it comes to melding our lives together. These are ideas formed before we even knew it was happening. They were formed when we were told to be 'good girls' while boys ran around feral and everyone just sighed and said, 'Well, boys will be boys.' Our space in this world as little girls was tightly ringfenced, while the boys were given free rein. We watched our mums make dinner while our dads read the paper.

I'm not suggesting that, on some deep, cellular level, we

are all just Suzy Homemakers desperate to perfect a soufflé while our men walk in at 6pm, a couple of drinks down, with a wad of cash in their pockets, and that we've just become swept up in a trend of equality thanks to a few bra-burners from back in the 60s. Not. At. All. But it is possible that we are, potentially, holding on to the final echo of old-school concepts about what men and women are and should be. When you put your ruby slippers on and look behind the curtain of respectability that you've set up in your soul, are those things true? Or are there some vintage values hanging around, dusty and long-forgotten, but made so well and solidly, back in the day, that they're almost impossible to recognise, let alone change? Behind the squares we post on Instagram, pink backgrounds with red letters, shouting feminist truisms, is there a part of us that thinks, no, *feels*, 'But it would be nice to just be able to be a mum'?

I make the distinction because that gap between what we truly believe and the founding beliefs that were bestowed upon us like an unwanted crown in early childhood is where the tension exists. It's where those niggling feelings squirm around in your gut. It's where the resentments grow and breed like fatal bacteria designed to poison all relationships in your midst. You *want* to want to be a career woman, because who doesn't? It's 2025, for God's sake! You're a feminist. You believe in equal rights. You can't just talk the talk, you have to walk the walk. But, also, there's an itchy feeling that maybe what *you* want, on an individual level, is to be a stay-at-home mum, too.

The same can be said the other way around. Perhaps you are a stay-at-home mum. Perhaps, outwardly, you truly believe that womanhood and caretaking are synonymous and that doing that makes you happy. There's absolutely nothing wrong with that, but if that's accompanied by a similar niggling feeling that says you could be doing something else as well, then there's a disconnect between what we want to believe we believe and what we have been hardwired to believe.

Much like those second-wave white upper- and middle-class feminists, who failed to include working-class women and women of colour in the fight, I am also guilty of succumbing to patriarchal hardwiring and forgetting to turn back and reach out to the women with less privilege than myself. I was no more than ten or eleven years old when I was excluding my mum from conversations that my dad and I would have in the car, but something in me was acting on a subconscious belief, that what was meant for me, as the next generation, wasn't my mother's purview. If I'm *really* honest, it was worse than that. If I'm *really* honest, I think a part of me blamed her for her own lack of opportunities, pitied her even. Even when I was still a child, society had started to groom me, getting me ready to step into a pseudo-equal society that played one female generation against another while ensuring our continued resentment. It also served to distract us from the fact that we were too busy fighting against each other to realise our lack of agency in a world that we held on our backs while men walked around it with diamonds on the soles of their shoes.

There was never any doubt in my mind that I would grow up, get married and have a family, just as my mother had done. I also didn't doubt that I would go to university, forge a career, be successful and live the 'have-it-all' dream – things my mother never had the chance to do. It didn't matter that

I didn't know a single woman who had achieved that. My mum hadn't been able to make it work, my mum's friend was a teacher but her husband was a doctor and there was never a night where she didn't put a three-course meal on the table and struggle with an addiction to sleeping tablets. Most of my friends' mums didn't work at all. A lot of them were divorced. Even if I really try, I can't think of one woman from my childhood that proved I could have a family and a career and be happy. And that's where the genius of the patriarchy lay. It relied on us wanting, so badly, for it to be possible, that we willingly turned a blind eye to the contrary evidence in front of us.

I didn't really ever learn the difference between 'mother' and 'martyr'. I come from a long line of martyrs and let me tell you – that's a lifestyle choice. It's not easy to break free from the comfort of believing that you are a better person than everyone else, but trust me, it's necessary. I used to say things like, 'He wouldn't survive without me,' and 'I don't know how he gets through the day when I'm not there.' Sure, a lot of this was said in jest, but of course there was the hard kernel of truth within it all. I genuinely believed that I was better, more evolved, more selfless, more giving than he was. *Without me,* I thought, *the whole fucking thing would fall apart.*

I used to talk about this in a way that made it sound like I wished it was different, that I didn't have to be the one who everyone relied on to get anything done, but the reality was, I loved that role. I loved falling on my mop-shaped sword, lying prone and exhausted at the feet of my charges, telling them it was my job to make sure they have everything they need. The 'I put myself last and do everything for everybody else and no one seems to give a shit' line was my sonic boom in any argument. It was almost as if I did it so that I had it to use as a weapon when conflict arose. It never occurred to me that I might not need such a destructive weapon if I didn't do it and hold it over the heads of all the people I lived with, but it was the only MO I'd ever seen.

The hugely uncomfortable truth is that the words 'martyr' and 'manipulator' are almost synonymous in this context. We don't consciously use our selfless acts maliciously to make the people we live with feel terrible about themselves, but as women, we realise pretty early on that playing the martyr card is a seriously effective – if only temporary – strategy.

While we could sit our partners and/or our kids down and explain calmly why we aren't feeling valued or 'kept in mind', we often don't. Instead, we wait until we are about to combust with rage after silently seething and sighing and tutting our way through the domestic chores for weeks. Then, in a furious flourish, we dust off our cross, hammer our hands and feet to the wood and present the bloody mess to our partners to shock them into realising, for the first time, just how hard we are working on their behalf.

Of course, what this looks like in real life is us losing our shit. It's screaming and shouting and crying accompanied by tortured monologues of how awful everyone that we live with is, how selfish they are, how thoughtless and uncaring. It's a shock tactic that probably works for about a week before the sad status quo resumes and the whole sorry show is repeated in approximately six to eight weeks' time. I didn't invent this cycle. I saw it. I learned it. I played it out over and over again because I'd seen my mother play it out time and time again, because her mother played it out and so on. I truly believe it's our generation's job to break this cycle.

I also inherited a serious case of generational 'control-freakitis'. When you think about it, it's a very normal response for those of us who grew up in the 80s and 90s, where emotional safety was a bit thin on the ground. Our parents did the best they could, but a lot of them didn't fully understand that making their kids feel safe was about more than putting a roof over their heads and making sure they had clean clothes. I can only speak to my own experience, but I was never told that making mistakes was okay, that it was human to not be perfect. It wasn't made explicitly clear to me that I would still be loved and valued even if I came home with the occasional B or C grade. Keeping up appearances was more than a TV show in the 80s and 90s; it was a programme for living. As long as everything looks okay, then everything *is* okay, and how everything looked on the outside was controlled so tightly that we mistook control for contentment.

It was only when I was married with kids that I realised how stupid I'd been. Pre-kids, it had been fine, good even. Not great – my husband and I had our fair share of 'why don't you fucking clean up after yourself' arguments – but, dare I say it, aside from the housework, I quite enjoyed being in charge of the life admin. It won't surprise you to know that, in my past life, I was a control freak, and so it suited me that I got to choose where we went on holiday, what car we drove, what sofas we bought, what presents we chose for friends and family, what we ate, where we ate. I've unpacked a lot of that in therapy since, but without children in the mix, bearing the mental load meant I got to make all the decisions.

I was good at it, and I took pride in that. As you can see, my blinkers hadn't yet been fully removed.

I realise now that the constant tension between wanting my partner to help with the mental load but also knowing he's never going to fold the towels in the right way, or organise the fridge properly when he puts the shopping away, or know what goes in the dryer and what doesn't, gave me a perfect excuse to put my hand to my forehead and dive headfirst in the puddle of self-pity. It also did nothing to make Jimmy *want* to help me. I was a toxic, micro-managing boss – and, make no mistake, I did see myself as the boss. I saw the house as business and Jimmy as an employee who I wished I could just fire because, in my mind, he was so fucking useless. There was no part of me that thought he might benefit from a bit of onboarding, or training for a job he'd never been primed to take on.

Whether we like it or not, we are the products of a generation that taught girls one set of life skills and boys another. How many of us women were taught to change tyres when we were little? How many of us were taught to fix a broken radio or learn how an engine works?* How many of us rely on our male partners to do the 'blue jobs' (God, I *hate* that term)? Of course, some girls were taught those things, but

---

* Sidenote: When I turned seventeen, I discovered that my godfather, Ian, had left me around £3,500 in his will. I decided to use this to buy a car – a red Vauxhall Corsa. My dad agreed to let me but only on the condition that I learned how to change a tyre, replace the spark plugs, change the oil and know where to put screen wash. I'd like to say I felt empowered by this but, honestly, I just felt resentful and, embarrassingly, always reverted to a man to help me with the car when something went wrong. So, I guess that's my part in reinforcing the patriarchal stereotypes as well.

many weren't, and I suspect those who weren't would be infuriated to be labelled thoughtless, selfish or incompetent when we assumed our male partners might just take care of that stuff. Whether I liked it or not, I had to accept my world the way it was and not the way I wished it was. And, by default, I had to accept that while I *wished* my husband just knew what the mental load was and all that it encapsulated, he didn't. That we were in this situation wasn't the fault of either of us individually, but now that we were here, stuck in the marital quagmire of mundane responsibility, we both needed to do something about it.

And then the children came, and that's when I called time on the set of my very own *Truman Show*. I realised it had been a facade, a stage set built on rotten foundations, and when it came crumbling down it was violent and shameful. All this time, I thought I'd been nailing it. I'd thought I was capable of, perhaps even occasionally exceptional at, spinning the plates, but that was utter bollocks. I was very far from capable of having it all, let alone doing it all. Managing the mental load for myself and another grown human was one thing. Being responsible for the labour that comes with two small children was a Goliath-sized task and when I, David, looked down at my hands, I discovered I couldn't find my slingshot and the kids had lost the stones anyway.

What was the effect of this? I'd love to say that I was able to philosophise about why this seismic shift had occurred and what it meant. I wish I could have looked at society as a whole and recognised that the problem wasn't me. But that's not what happened. What happened was that my confidence was ripped from me, my serenity was stolen, my mental health disintegrated. I sank into a postnatal depression, addiction, and my marriage almost fell apart because the only answer, as far as I could see it, was that I was broken, faulty, useless. I believed I'd been coddled all my life and told I was beautiful and smart and capable of achieving great things, only to be kneecapped by the most natural job of a woman: motherhood. As a woman, you can get comfortable with the fact that you may not be great at sports, or maths, or ironing, but to feel like you're not good at *motherhood*? That thing that should be intrinsic and instinctive within all of us? Well, that's a one-way trip to a total and utter lack of self-worth.

When the children arrived, I felt trapped. I was so angry – seething – but I didn't realise it. I just thought it was natural to feel this way with two small children and a husband that worked away a lot, and that I was just really bad at dealing with it. The irony that I had finally managed to emulate, perfectly, the version of my mother from all those years earlier, was completely lost on me. I wouldn't come to understand how much I'd ended up like my mother until many years later, and I'm grateful to say that with that realisation came a compassion for her that allowed me to let go of any and all resentments I had held against her.

It was only through my work online that I began to realise that the problem was not, in fact, me. Well, not entirely. It wasn't my *fault* that the stealthy destruction of women's mental health was a pandemic that no one was talking about, at least not loudly enough, but it was my responsibility – and my husband's – to address this imbalance within my own life. Since then, it's become a passion of mine to shine a light on it whenever I can. I'm not the only one. There are some incredible women and men shouting about the mental load and its consequences in creative, hilarious, educational and inspirational ways. This book is my way of throwing my two pence into the mix because, as King Mufasa says, 'The time has come.'

3

He Had Three Nipples and a Shoulder He Could Dislocate

'It was the best of times; it was the worst of times.'
– *A Tale of Two Cities*, Charles Dickens

Jimmy and I met at a gig. I know, I know, it's so clichéd. I got with one of the band. It's almost embarrassing, but there was something about him that intrigued me. On paper, we should have been fundamentally incompatible. He was ginger, from Birmingham, and a jobbing musician. I was a teacher who'd grown up in Yorkshire and always professed to never find redheads attractive. The night we met, the whites of my eyes were red, every blood vessel burst from a recent bout of gastroenteritis. I explained all this to Jimmy not knowing he had emetophobia – a fear of vomiting. He had three nipples and a shoulder he could dislocate at will. All this information was exchanged in mere minutes before we ended up snogging – and that, as they say, was that.

When I first met Jimmy, he was living in a flat in Belsize Park. It was actually a beautiful flat, but like most shared flats, it was rundown and unkempt and, dare I say it, not particularly clean. I didn't see any warning signs then, though. When you share a flat with friends, there's a weird 'hands-off' approach to the general upkeep of the communal spaces. So, while the kitchen was a bit grubby, and the floor in the living room looked like it had never been vacuumed, I just chalked it up to the reality of living with housemates. After all, I had also lived in a house-share and remembered constantly railing against the lack of accountability my housemates took when it came to keeping the living spaces clean. And yes, I'm going to say it: it was my male housemates that were the issue. The other girl I lived with and I battled with them constantly to help keep the kitchen and the living room clean. It was, slightly forebodingly, like we were speaking another language.

What should have been a glaring warning sign, however, was the state of Jimmy's room. As I write this, I'm not 100 per cent sure you'll get to read it because I suspect Jimmy will insist it's edited out, but his room should have been a sign of things to come. For Jimmy, his room was purely functional. It was a place to keep shit and sleep. That was it. His job meant he worked late nights, and during the day, he was out and about, so his room wasn't the calm, peaceful sanctuary I always made sure mine was. Instead, there was also a thin but complete layer of dust and cigarette ash. The sheets didn't appear to have been changed recently and the bed was never made. Golden Virginia tobacco flakes were left sprinkled over most surfaces and while the room didn't smell of body odour or dirty socks (of which there were many), it did hold on to the ghostly aromas of roll-ups.

At the time, I was an English teacher at Harrogate Grammar School, living in a little village called Starbeck. I shared a gorgeous house with one other girl called Charlotte, who was a PE teacher at another school in Harrogate. It was honestly one of the best times of my life. Charlotte was wonderful – she had a mega-watt smile and a laugh that was infectious and rarely silenced. She was laid-back and easy-going and, joy of all joys, we were *both* clean and tidy. That little terraced house in Starbeck felt like the first grown-up place I'd ever lived. During the week, we'd both buy fresh flowers and arrange them in vases on the heavy pine dining table and the mantlepiece. We'd light candles, fold each other's laundry and vacuum instinctively. It was truly one of the most harmonious living situations I've ever had.

And then, at the weekends, I would finish work on Friday and make the long drive down to London. I'd arrive at Jimmy's flat by about 9pm while he was out doing a gig. I would go to his room and immediately change the sheets, vacuum, dust all the cigarette ash off everything, collect his dirty laundry and pop it in the washer. I'd open the window and get some fresh air in and then I'd go to bed and wait for him to join me at about 2am, when we'd shag like rabbits. This was, of course, decades before the mental load was a coined phrase; possibly before women were even aware that it was a *thing* that we could question. It didn't occur to me that I could expect Jimmy to clean his room in anticipation of my arrival. It was a frighteningly easy instinct of mine to slip into the role of 'cleaner'. When I think about it now, is it possible I did it as a way of showing him, on a subconscious level, just how great I was and, even more embarrassingly, what a great wife I would make? It's not just possible; it's probably because *that's* what I thought women should be and what men wanted.

We did the long-distance thing for about four or five months before making plans to be closer together. I decided to try to get a job teaching in London, and when that happened I moved down into a shared house. It wasn't long before that shared house situation became a bit of a nightmare, and so we decided to move in together. We'd been going out less than a year before we started living together.

Things changed dramatically when we moved in together. Jimmy was the first boyfriend I had lived with. It's an important point to note, because I had absolutely no experience of the boy/girl co-habiting dynamic except for what I'd seen my mum and dad do, and even that was complicated by the addition of children – me. I'd never seen or experienced a man and a woman living together as a couple, on their own, so I had absolutely no idea what it was meant to look or feel like. I didn't know what boundaries were, let alone where to draw them, and even if I did, I wouldn't have had the confidence or the self-knowledge to know how to implement them. I was a baby and so was he and, on top of all that, we brought so much of our own baggage along with us that, with hindsight, I can see now that it wasn't a healthy situation.

In 2010, Jimmy and I were renting a flat in Willesden Green that was about the size of my big toenail. It cost us around £450 each a month. The mental load wasn't a concept either of us had ever considered, but it was almost immediately apparent that cohabiting wasn't going to be as joyful as I thought it would be.

I was in my mid-twenties and I'd watched enough rom-coms to know that living with your boyfriend was supposed to be fun and sex-filled and that Sunday mornings were about coffee and toast in bed with a mucky cuddle thrown in for good measure. In the movies, no one ever cleaned the shit stains off the loo, or filled and emptied the dishwasher. There was never any laundry hanging off every available surface to dry. It was just white crumpled sheets, perfect lighting and stylish interiors.

On the other hand, I don't think Jimmy had ever seen a rom-com in his life. To me, it felt like Jimmy saw this move as just another shared house situation rather than the start of a beautiful life together, which was how I saw it. Sure, I'd cleaned his room when we were dating and spending the weekends together, but I assumed (my first mistake) that because this was *our* room and not *his* room, that he would take more care with it. Spoiler alert: he didn't. Did we consider having a conversation about what this move meant to us? Did we bollocks. Communication, dear reader, as I'm sure you're beginning to see, was not our strong suit.

I entered into the situation thinking it was the most romantic thing I'd ever done, so you can imagine my disappointment when I realised it was the exact opposite. I think if my expectations hadn't been so high, if the lies I'd lapped up about relationships weren't so ingrained in me, if I'd been a little more grown up about the whole thing and less aware of the sheltered life I'd lived, it might have been an easier transition. Instead, I felt angry and disappointed in the way that only an unmet expectation can conjure. Our lack of ability to really connect on a domestic, shared-space level was actually quite impressive. I got angry a lot, and I can honestly say it didn't occur to me to dig beneath the easy-to-access feelings like anger or frustration, because I'd never seen that happen. I thought that it was normal for women to spend their lives frustrated about living with a man. I never, ever considered that it could be different, despite wishing it was, and so I resorted to all the tricks I'd seen my mum use – silence, door slamming, 'I'm fine' on repeat. The usual.

It wasn't all bad, of course; we loved each other and had a lot of fun. We had a great group of friends and very little responsibility. Our sex life was good and even though we didn't have loads of money, our bills were always paid and we were able to eat out a lot thanks to a £10-per-person, three-course-meal-and-a-bottle-of-wine deal at a little restaurant by Willesden Green tube station called The Little Star. But there was always an undercurrent of him not meeting my expectations when it came to being a partner on a domestic level and him wishing I would relax, stop nagging and worrying about what other people thought all the time.

The resentments grew around my heart like Japanese knotweed squeezing the life out of a building's foundations. I didn't know it then, but the seeds were sown. The little roots of bitterness had started to take hold on the deepest, darkest, most unexplored parts of our consciousness. We were trudging blindly down the well-worn paths of gender roles and expectations upon which generations before us had blazed the trail. The problem is, of course, that those paths don't run next to each other. At some point they veer violently away from each other until you have to scream at the top of your voice to be in with a chance of being heard.

I hated that I lived with a boy-shaped human who just didn't *see* the shit that I saw. He didn't see the piss stains on the loo seat or on the floor (how, *how* do they get it on the floor? Isn't the toilet big enough?), or maybe he did, but they didn't elicit the same anxiety in him that they did in me, the same need to grab the bleach and clean it up immediately. The rage wasn't just because I appeared to be the resident skivvy; it was also because I'd thought it would be something completely different. *An expectation is a resentment waiting to happen*, and honestly, this was the perfect example of that.

Here's what I couldn't understand: I didn't do all the cleaning because I *wanted* to clean up after him or because I enjoyed it. I did it because I didn't want to live in a shit hole. And it wasn't even just a cleanliness thing. At some point, in my childhood, the state of the house had become inextricably linked to the state of my mental health, the levels of my anxiety. I'd seen my mum lose her shit on numerous occasions because the house wasn't just right and, in a society like ours, when a house isn't right then it's the woman that's wrong. When a house was messy and unkempt it was the woman of the house that was judged and found wanting. So, monkey see, monkey do, or, perhaps more accurately, mummy see, mummy do. Therefore, my desire for it to be clean and for him to tidy up after himself wasn't just about me wanting to live in a show home. It was about me doing all I could to fulfil the expectations I felt everyone had of me – to be a great homemaker, the queen of a clean house.

Mess and dirt didn't affect Jimmy in the same way. A house was a thing, functional, and as long as it had four walls and a roof, it served its purpose. For me, my home was my sanctuary, my safe place, and it never occurred to us to have a conversation about this. It was clear in my own head that I was running around cleaning everything because it was too dirty for me to feel comfortable in, perhaps even *safe* in, but I suspect the message Jimmy received was, 'Cat will clean up my mess and it seems like she enjoys doing it,' and honestly, I can't blame him.

I think, on reflection, this miscommunication continued for many years. I did the cleaning because I didn't want to live in a dirty house; he thought I did it because I liked it. I don't think you can underestimate the toxic power of a narrative we make up in our own heads because we think we know what someone else is thinking or feeling. For us, it was the poison that infected the life-blood of our connection. I made up a narrative that portrayed him as a thoughtless, selfish, lazy arsehole. He made up a narrative that portrayed me as a controlling fun-sponge with unrealistic expectations and a mean tongue. Daily, we unconsciously searched for evidence to prove those narratives true and, inevitably, we could always find it.

I remember our bedroom window was so close to the train line in Willesden Green that I could practically hand a cup of tea to the engineers while they worked with their pneumatic drills on the tracks between the hours of midnight and 4am. I remember complaining relentlessly to our friends with kids about how tired we were because of the work they were doing on the train tracks, and I honestly can't believe none of them punched us in the face as their toddlers ran around finding sharp corners with their heads and their babies cried and cried and cried while they cooked Sunday lunch for us, having managed to get forty-seven minutes' sleep the night before.

To say we were clueless is an understatement. We were, more accurately, insufferable. We were totally and mind-numbingly ignorant about the parallel reality that our friends – three couples that all had kids – were living, with bills, kids, school fairs, homework, laundry, dental appointments and the endless to-do list of other things.

Even if we could have stretched our tiny, self-centred brains far enough to consider those things, we would never have been able to imagine the role the mental load played in exacerbating all those things for them, and especially the women, because the mental load isn't stuff you can see and touch. The mental load isn't just about *doing* all the stuff. The mental load is constantly *thinking* about having to do all the stuff, and then, when you forget to do some of the stuff, the mental load is also about beating yourself up about that, while still trying to keep in mind all the other stuff you've got to do. It's a relentless mental marathon with no wee breaks, a 24/7 night shift with no holiday days or sick days. And so, Jimmy and I would turn up at our friends' houses, drink their wine, eat the food they put in front of us, play with their kids a bit and then leave, and it never, ever occurred to us that, behind the scenes, they were drowning in overwhelm or murderous with resentment or, probably, both. It was only after we'd had our own children and told them how hard we were finding it that they told us they'd been through the same feelings. *Why didn't you tell us?* we'd lament. *You can't really understand it until you're in it*, they'd reply, and they were right.

To give Jimmy and I *some* credit – they all hid it well. Every single one of them made it look like they had their domestic ducks in a row. There was absolutely no indication that they were hanging on by a thread, so what else was there for us to do except get married and have children? And so, on 24 August 2011, in a beautiful room in Marylebone Town Hall, Jimmy and I got legally married in front of two of our friends, Nick and Sarah. We celebrated in a pub in Chiswick before taking it to Soho House to spend our first night as a married couple together. On 3 September, just a week later, we did the whole wedding thing for real in France, in front of eighty of our nearest and dearest, and – I can say this with unwavering honesty – it was the best day of my life.

I know that people roll their eyes when I say that, and I get it, but there is something truly magical about the people you love most in the world coming together to celebrate you and your person, with nothing but joy in their heart and a smile on their face. It didn't matter what the place settings looked like, or what shoes I was wearing. None of that turned out to be important in the slightest. What was important was everyone jumping in the pool at midnight, the photos that captured expansive smiles on our friends' and family's faces, my dad accidentally stepping on my veil and nearly taking me down as we walked down the aisle, the way mine and Jimmy's hands shook with the enormity of what we were doing as we placed the rings on each other's fingers. If I'd had any doubts about whether Jimmy was the man for me, the way I felt on the day I married him dispelled any and all of them.

To this day, I think it's holding on to that feeling that got us through the worst of times.

Inevitably, and I'm laughing as I type this, it was downhill from there. It was inevitable, because neither of us had a fucking clue what it meant to be married. We didn't know it was about being a team. We didn't know it was 90 per cent about the hard graft through the minutiae of daily life. We didn't know it was more about a cup of tea in the morning than a 5-star holiday every year. We didn't know it was about catching each other's eye and sharing a smile rather than having wild sex every night. We didn't know it was about accepting each other at our worst rather than always trying to be perfect. We were children; children with no useful instructions as to how to do marriage well. We were playing the roles we thought we should play, and when one or both of us slipped out of character, the whole facade exploded in our faces.

When our eldest, Billie, arrived, we had survived two years of marriage, buying a house and almost renovating it. I'd definitely been the driving force behind getting pregnant and, once again, here we were, at the beginning of an experience we thought we knew how to handle but were woefully underprepared for. Despite the hours of NCT classes, the books read, the parenting forums joined, we had no fucking clue what parenthood had in store for us and it hit us both in ways we could never have imagined.

I think a lot of people are guilty of glossing over the epically transformational, torturous experience becoming a parent can be. It's not because we willingly lie about what it was like. It's because no one has ever made space for new parents to have that conversation safely. No one has ever considered the need to debrief new parents and reassure them that their experience was valid. We lie in the bed we made, and even though that bed has broken springs, is covered in baby sick and peppered with the occasional damp patch, we pull the covers up to our necks, smile and pretend that everything is fine; and in the morning, we get up and make the bed, being sure to hide the swamp fest it's become. We throw a thin gauze of respectability over the bleeding, the pain, the sleeplessness, the helplessness, the timelessness of it all.

Why do we gloss? Why do we pretend it's how we want it to be, rather than how it really is? I think it has a lot to do with the portrayal of families and relationships in everything we consume: adverts, books, songs, TV shows, magazines and movies. They sell us fairy tales about what a good relationship and a happy life looks like. Those fairy tales are, to put it simply, total and utter bollocks, and while I know you know that in your rational brain, I don't think we're as aware as we should be of the way those toxic tales have embedded themselves into the very fibre of our souls. I can't emphasise enough how important it is for us to pull back the curtain on popular culture and the lies it's sold us – because it's this that will start to set us free.

4

The Rom-Con

'Deceive not thyself by overexpecting happiness in the married estate . . . Remember the nightingales which sing only some months in the spring, but commonly are silent when they have hatched their eggs.' – Thomas Fuller

Like many of you, I grew up watching rom-coms. *Sleepless in Seattle, When Harry Met Sally, How to Lose a Guy in 10 Days, My Best Friend's Wedding* . . . the list goes on and on. These films were, in some ways, the preview to social media. These movies were the first things I would compare my own relationship to and inevitably come out on the losing side. No matter how hard I tried, I couldn't seem to find a man who behaved like the men in the movies. I couldn't seem to be as funny or as effortlessly beautiful as the women. The sheer volume of these romantic comedies that I simultaneously lapped up because I loved them, but also hated because they made me feel less than, meant that the version of love they presented was hardwired into me.

In the early days of my relationship with Jimmy, this false narrative tripped me up almost daily. I so desperately wanted him to chase me down the street when I stormed off. When I cried quietly into my pillow (but loud enough for him to hear) after a fight, I wanted him to turn over, take me in his arms and whisper *sorry* into my ear. Instead, he'd go to sleep. I wanted him to stand up through the sunroof of his car, grasping a bunch of red roses and declare his undying love for me in an embarrassing public display of affection. It didn't matter that his car didn't have a sunroof nor that he simply told me he loved me every day. I wanted the glamour of it all; my insecurity needed the performative displays of love that I'd seen on the big screen. Anything less felt pedestrian.

Stream any rom-com and you'll find that the man just knows what to say when the woman is sad or struggling. He'll turn up with flowers just *because* (insert vomming emoji here), they'll never have laundry hanging around the house because the tumble dryer is broken and they have a very healthy sex life. They'll listen to each other, apologise to each other and do all they can to make each other feel kept in mind. Oh, and they'll both always look absolutely incredible. You'll never see him scratching his arse in a pair of boxers with one testicle hanging out of the hole that's slowly but surely appeared and you'll never see her with greasy hair scraped up in a bun, in a pair of old joggers with the VPL of her period pants clearly visible.

And that, ladies and gentlemen, is the rom-con. It's the big, fat pack of lies that Hollywood has sold us throughout the years. It's the bollocks that every ballad has stuffed down our throat since, well, men have been trying to stuff themselves down our throats. It's the romance novels, the soap operas, the porn. It's the fantasies, very loosely based on facts, that have somehow superseded the reality of what a relationship is and what it looks and feels like.

It's the same when it comes to sex. The mucky cuddles. The shagging, the banging, the making of the beast with two backs. The horizontal refreshment, the getting laid, the act of darkness, the Netflix and chilling, the knocking of the boots, the humping, the fucking, the hiding of the sausage. The smashing, the banging, the tangoing, the flinging, the shaking of the sheets. Call it whatever you like – somehow, somewhere along the line, sex has become the most important identifier when it comes to a 'good' marriage or relationship.

And brace yourself for an unpopular opinion, because I'm calling bullshit. In my opinion, when it comes to a good relationship, sex is a nice-to-have but absolutely not a necessity. Surely, we can all agree that there are as many features of a good relationship as there are good relationships? To suggest that every relationship between every human must include a passionate and regular sex life seems bonkers to me. We are at a point where couples are embarrassed to admit that they don't have very much sex, or indeed any at all, when it makes biological sense that as you get older and closer to surpassing your fertile years, your desire for sex will inevitably and naturally decrease.

In the same way that we have superimposed the social construct of 'love' onto the biological and evolutionary inclinations of partnerships, we have also done the same with sex. Almost fifty and *not* having sex at least once a week? Society thinks there's something wrong with you. Nature, on the other hand, is probably suggesting that you relax a little, chill out, let your body recover from the rigours that being a sexual and reproductive being has had on you over the last three decades. Find and feel intimacy in other ways, like *actually* Netflixing and chilling without letting a probing penis ruin your true crime documentary. Hold hands, share a secret joke whispered into each other's ear, touch feet while you fall asleep next to each other.

Sex isn't intimacy. I've had many sexual encounters that felt anything other than intimate. Having sex and being connected are not the same thing *unless* you are connected on an emotional level first. That doesn't mean that sex without intimacy can't be fun – in fact, that's often all it is. The kind of sex you have when you first meet someone that comes with the fanny flutters, the pelvic shivers, the dampness – that's fucking great. It's addictive and leaves you heady with emotion, but it doesn't listen when you talk or catch you when you fall. It doesn't care if the dishwasher is empty or how your day was. It just cares about when it can get going again and feel that feeling again. It's primal and intense and it burns brightly but fades quickly.

Sex for men is an act. Sex for women is a feeling. Men 'do' sex and women feel it. Feeling turned on isn't a switch that we can flip in the same way that it seems to be for men and, when it comes to the mental load, the truth is this:

Women don't want to have sex with men they have to look after, pick up after and clean up after. Women aren't turned on by a lack of recognition, nor do they get wet with underappreciation. We don't want to 'put out' if your dirty socks aren't 'put in' the laundry basket.

To be very clear – sex is not a reward for vacuuming without being asked. You do not get a medal or a blowjob. What we jokingly refer to as 'choreplay' is not that transactional. As with most things, it's more nuanced than that. The reward for vacuuming your own house is being seen, by your partner, as a grown-ass human who participates in the responsibility of looking after his own house. The extra perks of being seen by your partner as a grown-ass human is that your partner feels respected, appreciated, valued and emotionally safe. That, unsurprisingly, makes you more attractive to your partner. The bonus of being more attractive is that your partner is more likely to shag you. Your capability as a thoughtful and respectful human being is what makes you attractive. Being a man who doesn't need managing, directing, following around, is what makes you attractive, and when that happens, then we're more likely to get fizzy knickers.

Despite what the movies tell us, the mental load does exist in every relationship and it often feels like a wrecking ball that we just about managed to dodge, a pendulum that, with great effort, we can still temporarily. Because the mental load never, ever ends. Even if we spend the whole day getting to grips with the mental load, there's little sense of satisfaction at the end of it. The mental load is not a Super Mario video game that we can complete, never to have to deal with again. Instead, it's like a never-ending game of Tetris where all the falling pieces are things on our to-do list and we desperately hope that the long piece comes at the right time so that we can clear four lines in one go. More often than not, though, the long piece doesn't come, or it comes but we miss it because one of the other pieces was sick or shouting for a snack, and the whole thing gets on top of us until we die. But we don't die for ever; there's no eternal rest for us. We die only to be brought back from the dead and told to do it all over again.

For women, sex is internal. It's an invasion and, when consensual, it's a welcome one, but an invasion it still is. It's an act of us opening ourselves up physically, and this is inextricably linked to an emotional opening up as well. Having sex for women is an enormous act of vulnerability, trust and courage. We can be hurt physically and emotionally all at the same time and there is not a moment when that fact is not lost on us, even during the act itself, even if it's not conscious. It's not like that for men. Sex for men is an external pursuit. It's an act you perform *on someone*, whereas for women, it's something that is *done to us*.

Switching from managing domestic Tetris to being a freak between the sheets is not as easy as anyone wants it to be . . . especially if those sheets haven't been changed in two weeks. Yes, we don't forget the time you forgot the kids' doctor's appointment three weeks ago, but we also don't forget the time you took care of changing the beds last month. We carry these things with us, not because we are sadistic little dictators who want to shame you at any given time, but because these things *matter* to us, these things make us feel safe and when we feel safe, then and *only then* can we enjoy sex. When the things that matter to us are ignored or disregarded, then sex becomes nothing more than another thing to add on our to-do list, another thing that takes from us rather than gives, and there's nothing sexy about that.

It's not just an emotional response. It's a physical one. When I spend the day at home, cleaning and getting on top of the life admin and the mental load, I can easily hit 19k steps. I've probably walked up and down the stairs twenty to thirty times. I've changed four beds* (which is about the equivalent of four HIIT sessions) and cooked three meals. I don't have the energy or the quads to bounce up and down on top of my husband at that point because, let's face it, that's what's happening. Not because he's selfish, but because I'm knackered and I know that's the quickest way to get the job done. That's where our heads go to when we're having sex because we feel like we have to rather than because we feel like we want to.

Women need men to know that when we say we're 'too tired' or we've 'got a headache' it's absolutely because we are 100 per cent knackered and dehydrated to the point of dying from picking up after the people we live with all day. There isn't a woman in the world who cleans skid marks off the toilet bowl and thinks, *God, I just want to sit on the face of the man who made these marks.* Not one woman. And I don't need to do any scientific research to back that up.

So, while society has bombarded us with what a relationship *should* look like, and thrown love and passion to the forefront, we have forgotten that there is a biological and

---

* On the subject of beds, can we please take a moment to discuss bunk beds? I am certain, with every *single* fibre of my being that a man invented bunk beds. If the man who designed these devil-structures had considered the physical act of having to change the sheets on a bunk bed, he would have burned his blueprints. When you change the top bunk, you fear for your life and collect more than a few scrapes in the process. When you change the bottom bunk, you hit your head so many times you invariably emerge with a mild concussion. Can we start a petition to ban all bunk beds? What's wrong with a trundle bed?

evolutionary blueprint for a relationship between a man and a woman. At the most basic level, we are designed to behave and act in a certain way in relationships so that we continue the human race. Beyond that, from a scientific point of view (and please note, I use the word scientific very loosely), the reward for doing that isn't the skewed perception of relational success that we refer to as 'love'. It's actually care, protection, kindness and support. It's a mate – a friend, a partner, another human being – you can rely on to keep you in mind and vice versa.

Here's what I think: rom-cons have done us women dirty. The concept of love that we've developed in recent centuries is a toxic one that has, at best, given us unreasonably high expectations of any human being and at worst, kneecapped our self-esteem. Whenever I watch shows like *Married at First Sight* and *Love Is Blind*, I'm always infuriated and saddened at the same time when I hear a contestant say something along the lines of 'I want what my parents have. They've been married for thirty years and they love each other so much.'

Yeah, good luck with that, Deidre. Do you think that's what it was always like? Do you think your parents woke up every day in a haze of blissful love after banging each other's brains out all night? Do you think they didn't go through times where they questioned their life choices or wondered if they had the balls to leave each other? Do you think your mum didn't spend time fantasising about running off with the fit mechanic who just serviced her car because 'at least he fucking noticed her?' Or that your dad didn't wish he could run away and leave all the responsibility far behind him? Do you honestly believe your mum wasn't riddled with resentment when your dad left his dirty socks near, but not inside, the laundry bin? Or that your dad dreamed of a life with a woman who didn't nag him to put the sodding loo seat down all the time?

I know now that staying together for thirty years doesn't happen because you're in love in the way that Hollywood tells you that you should be. It happens because you woke up every day and *chose* to not leave the person lying next to you *despite* the fact that they're sometimes annoying and messy and thoughtless, because guess what? They're also human and, unless they truly are a c*nt, they are probably trying their best, and if they're not, but they're also still not a c*nt, then they're probably decent enough to sit down and have a conversation with you about it.

Because love in the way that Hollywood and Ed bloody Sheeran presents it isn't real life.

Love isn't a real thing that can be defined. Love isn't ripping each other's clothes off. It's not showering your partner with gifts or whisking them off on surprise trips. Love isn't wearing matching outfits or just knowing what you're thinking and feeling. No – none of that is love. That's just some of the fun 'nice-to-haves' in a relationship. That's love with privilege.

I spent so many years resenting the men I was with because they didn't live up to my expectations of what true love was. I'm sure I didn't live up to their expectations either – wherever those may have come from (porn?). I had no idea that what I saw in movies, on TV and in books wasn't love. I didn't know it was the same fairy tale in various different guises and it skewed my perspective so much that I couldn't help but feel deeply unsatisfied with every relationship I was in.

It's taken me hours of couples' therapy, even more hours of observing other couples and relationships, three years of sobriety (and counting), numerous fights and come-to-Jesus chats with my husband and a huge dollop of self-reflection to realise that love is something very different. Love is an internal quietness and calmness. Love is knowing that they've kept me in mind when it comes to any decision they've made. Love is accepting that I am responsible for my own happiness and not relying on someone else to do that for me. It's also about committing to not getting in the way of my partner's happiness and to do all I can to support it, while not being the source of it all.

Ironically, I think a kind of telepathy does exist between us now, but that's not because there was some cosmic connection from the outset that merged our consciousnesses. It's because we've been through so much shit as a couple. It's because we've got each other wrong *so many times* and worked through it and come back together that we've grown to understand each other on a level that can only come through years of doing our best.

I cannot underestimate the role that the mental load played in that development. It was the biggest source of tension in our marriage, certainly from my side. It was at the root of all the messy, spiky, uncomfortable feelings I had about our relationship. It infected everything, including our sex life. The mental load was like a herpes virus in our marriage. It would disappear for a while, no visible signs of it identifiable, until it broke out suddenly. Sure, there were some warning signs – tiredness, a tingling of resentment, some pain – but it was hard to know exactly when it was going to rear its ugly head again. There was also no cure because there was no *getting rid* of the mental load. It was always a case of learning to manage it in a responsible way that didn't hurt anyone else. It was only in couples' therapy that Jimmy and I were finally able to see the impact it had on our connection with each other.

So, if you're itching to exit stage left from your partnership because you keep comparing your relationship to the ones you see on screens or read about in books, then take a minute and pause. When I sat Jimmy down and told him we were separating, I remember saying, 'If we could work things out then you're the person I'd always choose, but I just think it's gone too far; I don't think we can come back from this.' Despite all the pain and resentment I held towards him, there was part of me that was still able to acknowledge that, in an ideal world, I'd still choose him, but I just couldn't see a way through. Thankfully, he convinced me to go back to couples' therapy, and that marked the beginning of a long slog back to each other. Much of that slog was about identifying our unreasonable expectations of each other and what a marriage was and breaking them down and replacing them with more forgiving and more realistic models that we weren't destined to fall short of from the start.

5

Girl on Tour

'I'm just a small part of a big world, and I don't know where I belong.' – *The Perks of Being a Wallflower*, Stephen Chbosky

In 2010, I left my career as a secondary-school English teacher in inner-city London schools to tour the world with an iconic rock star as his production assistant. Teaching, in many ways, remains a true vocation of mine. I loved being in the classroom. I loved the kids and, yes, they were challenging, but I loved that challenge. My unfiltered honesty was as present then as it is today and I think that my willingness to share with students some of the things I struggled with, to admit that I wasn't some paragon of virtue who knew everything, to give them room to express themselves, to talk to them as if they weren't the lizard-brained, hormone-fuelled liabilities that they really were, enabled me to connect with them. I wasn't a perfect teacher by any means, but I think a lot of my students would say they remember me fondly. Many of them have been in touch via social media since, and seeing who they grew up to be (one is a successful journalist, another is a movie star) is one of my true joys in life.

There was an ease with which I was able to do this. It was a decision unhindered by the friction of responsibility or commitments. Jimmy and I were renting a flat together but at this point we weren't married. I had the luxurious naivety of youth on my side. I didn't want to teach anymore, therefore I stopped teaching, and despite everyone telling me I was making a mistake, it didn't occur to me to listen. I saw Jimmy work in the music industry and it looked like a lot of fun. Being self-employed also looked like a blast, and so I thought I'd get a job in music. And with all the confidence of a man taking a selfie in the gym, that's what I did.

Jimmy always references this moment when he talks about how he fell in love with my ability to decide that something was going to be and make it so. It had taken him years of earning almost nothing, doing shit jobs in filthy bars and living on tinned carrots in a mouse-infested flat in Paddington before he was able to make a living from music. Understandably, he didn't have much faith in me being able to build a career in the music industry just because I'd suddenly decided that was what I wanted to do, and honestly, who can blame him?

A friend of ours was, at the time, drumming for a rock star from a very famous band from the 60s and 70s. He was doing a solo tour. The band had long since split up in the way that bands from that era did – dramatically, publicly and with more than a little shit-talk that, remarkably, still continues between them to this day.* The tour were having some issues with their

* Because I know you're desperate to know who it was, I want to be clear that the decision to anonymise it was a (probably wise) one made by the legal team and not by me. If you see me out and about, however, ask me and I might tell you ☺

production assistant and according to our mate, the tour manager was looking to replace her. They were doing a show the following week at the Royal Albert Hall in London and my friend suggested I come down and talk to the tour manager.

When the day came, I remember being really nervous.

Jimmy asked me if I knew of the musician I was going to be working for.

'Not really,' I confessed.

Jimmy looked embarrassed for me. 'You should probably give him a google before you go down there.'

It's fair to say that Jimmy's hopes weren't high, but I was undeterred. A quick google only confirmed that I *still* didn't know who he was. I'd grown up on Madonna's *Immaculate Collection* and a vinyl copy of Queen's *Greatest Hits* I'd picked up at a car boot sale. My parents weren't particularly musical or, indeed, into music. My mum always said she loved Neil Diamond but I never once heard her play any music, other than what was on Radio 2. My dad's musical preferences were slightly broader, but not much. He'd play John Denver and The Eagles on repeat in his car until, in a rather perverse turn of events, he decided he loved Right Said Fred. That was a tough year.

When I got to the Royal Albert Hall, the tour manager had forgotten I was coming, but out of courtesy to our mutual friend, he agreed to have a chat with me, despite having to deal with the production assistant, who was already clearly causing more problems than she was solving. I sat down opposite the tour manager, who looked harassed and more than a little irritated at having to give this random girl ten minutes of his time. We chit-chatted about what experience I had. *Absolutely none,* I told him, *but I learn quick and I work hard.*

'Well,' he said, looking distractedly towards the open door where a commotion appeared to be brewing in the corridor, 'you're not going to walk into a production assistant job, but I can use you for wardrobe here and there. How does that sound?'

It sounded bloody fantastic, and as I was about to tell him that, the production assistant spilled into the room. She was a tiny, pocket-sized human who appeared to have consumed the contents of a vodka bottle that wasn't much smaller than she was. I don't think she could have told you what city she was in, or which artist she was working for, and to say that the tour manager was displeased would be a gross understatement. He exploded from behind the desk, standing up so quickly his chair fell over.

'That's it!' he screamed. 'I've had it.' He gestured towards a security guard. 'Get her pass and get that c*nt out of here. I never want to see her again.' With that, the production assistant was disentangled from her AAA pass and removed from the room. The tour manager righted his chair, sat down heavily, his round face red with rage, sweat dripping down his forehead. He sighed heavily and looked up at me resignedly.

'I know I said you weren't going to walk into a production assistant's job, but how do you fancy starting now?'

I was speechless. A minute ago, I was delighted to be given a 'here-and-there' wardrobe job. Now I was being offered a production assistant job?

'Erm . . .' I stammered, 'are you saying my first gig is at the Royal Albert Hall?'

'Yes, do you want it?'

'Sure.'

And with that he gave me the AAA pass, showed me where

the stage was, where the quick change was, what I was going to have to do during the show and then introduced me to the rock star. For the next three years, the tour manager took me under his wing and mentored me into a pretty fucking good production assistant, and to this day I remain grateful to him (and the drunk production assistant) for giving me that chance.

Working in the music industry was a culture shock, to say the least. Suddenly, there were no alarms in the morning or meetings with parents, or evening training sessions in the school hall. My life was no longer corralled within the confines of school holidays and weekends. Every day was a weekend and I spent those days in tour buses, or fancy hotels, drinking free booze on tap, earning a decent day rate, and being my own boss. I was living life in a way that few people get the chance to.

It turned out, though, that the joke was on me, because somewhere between flying business class to Los Angeles and being side of stage at the Royal Variety Performance, I had forgotten that I was, indeed, a woman, and worse, a woman of breeding age, and therefore subject to an entirely different set of restrictions to my male counterparts. The most signifi-cant of those male counterparts was, of course, my husband (boyfriend at the time), who was working as a touring session musician.

It soon became clear that my experience as a woman in the music industry was very different from that of my husband. The biggest difference was, actually, nothing to do with the mental load or the fact that I was a woman. It was because he was 'Talent' and I was 'Crew', or for those of you who haven't worked in the music industry, but have probably seen *Downton Abbey*: he was 'upstairs' and I was 'downstairs'.

There's a hierarchy on a tour that you step out of at your peril regardless of your gender – but there's a second, more insidious hierarchy in the music industry that is *all* about gender. In short, when I was working in it, it was an unapologetically misogynistic and, at times, frankly, unsafe industry for women to work in. I travelled around the world as the only woman in a crew of middle-aged men, who didn't think it at all inappropriate to comment on my outfit, my boobs or make sexual jokes aimed at me. It was banter, and honestly, at the time, I took it as banter. I wasn't aware enough to know it was wrong; I wasn't confident enough to challenge it; and I was way too grateful to have been given a seat on the tour bus at all to ever expect respect to be part of the deal. As a woman, in 2011, there was no doubt that I was in a man's world.

One night, I was in my bunk on the tour bus with my curtains closed – it's an unwritten rule that you don't disturb someone in their bunk with their curtains closed – when the front of house engineer, after a few drinks, decided to rip my curtains open and scream at me. He was upset that the tour manager and I had a Social Security number and therefore weren't subject to the same tax deductions that he was from earnings made touring America. He thought the tour manager and I had engineered it that way on purpose in a devious attempt to screw him over (as if we had the time or the capabilities to do such a thing). He scared the shit out of me when he threw his head and shoulders into my bunk. My bunk was supposed to be my safe space on that bus and now there was nowhere for me to go. I spent that night sobbing quietly, hoping no one would hear me. The next morning I got up, went into the venue and made sure everyone, including the front of house guy, had everything they needed. I never saw the front of house guy say a word to the male tour manager about his Social Security number.

My job as a production assistant (which is basically the tour manager's assistant and first point of contact for the talent) was largely seen as a job that, if a woman wanted to work in music, then this was the role for her. Men do it because there aren't enough women in the touring industry, but essentially, the role of production assistant is mental load manager, and if you see a female crew member and they're not hair and make-up, they're probably the production assistant.*

My Job Description as Production Assistant for an Iconic Rock Star

1. Talent
Ensure Talent has everything he needs *before* he needs it. Anticipate everything. Never leave him alone and whatever he wants, the answer is yes. You must spray his bald patch with hair dye to cover it. If he wants you to massage his legs at inappropriate times – say in TV green rooms – while other old white men look on and watch, then you must oblige. You

---

* At this point, I want to make it clear that I do know some women who are front of house engineers, or monitor engineers or lampies, or tour managers, but they are the exceptional few who through sheer fucking talent and a willingness to take on a lot of shit on the way have bust through the musical glass ceiling.

must iron twenty-four shirts before every show even though he wears the same three shirts every night. If you only iron those three shirts, he will insist on wearing another shirt. You must ensure you have his 'special drink' available and at the perfect temperature at any given moment. It is made from pineapple juice (organic), manuka honey (15+ at least) and fresh ginger. He will only want to drink it if he thinks you haven't made it. If you have made it and he doesn't drink it, you must not refrigerate it and heat it up for the next day. You must make a fresh batch, that he probably still won't drink. In hotels, you must answer the phone to him at any time of the day or night and fulfil his requests for food, or a massage, or a doctor to visit him in his hotel for a B12 shot. You must stand side of stage at every show and help him change in between songs and, at the end of the show, you must be there with a towel and water and ensure there is a bottle of red wine in his dressing room. Make sure he has a clean razor in the shower each night, fresh boxer shorts and socks, and that his girlfriend has everything she needs.

2. Band & Crew

Make sure all band and crew know what they are doing each day. They'll need this written down on a sheet with the day's itinerary written on it and emailed out to them the night before. They won't bother reading it because it'll just be much easier to ask you, so please ensure you have all the vital information in your head ready to give out to anyone and everyone who asks you. Screaming 'It's on the fucking day sheet' is not an acceptable answer. You are in charge of food, hot and cold drinks, ensuring everyone knows where they are going in the venue. Please place signs around every venue so that no one has to actually find their own way somewhere. If the band or crew forget anything or can't find something, then it is your responsibility to organise getting it from somewhere. This could be anything from cold and flu medicine to clean undies to a mouth organ in E. Also, please maintain a good sense of humour throughout, and if they slap you on the bum, remember, it's just bants.

The job wasn't all bad, by any means. I will always be eternally grateful to the tour manager, who took a punt on a girl with no experience in the industry but happened to be in the right place at the right time. I learned a lot, but mostly, I learned how to run a tight ship, how to juggle laundry and catering and schedules and transport because, really, that was pretty much the only role open to women in touring.

At this point, I didn't have any children, but Jimmy and I had just got married and we were both clear that getting me knocked up was the next step. I don't think the decision to have a baby was a particularly well-thought-out one – certainly not on my part – largely because I don't remember thinking it needed much thought. It was just what newly married couples did, right? I don't remember thinking about the possible impact being a mum with a real-life, actual baby might have on my career or my place in this world more generally. It definitely didn't occur to me that I couldn't do it all and have it all, and so with the enthusiasm of toddlers participating in their first sports day, Jimmy and I set about getting pregnant.

In January of 2013, I found out I was indeed going to have a baby. Instinctively I knew that it would be wise to keep this a secret from the tour manager and the rest of the team, but it wasn't long before they noticed I was turning down drinks and going to bed weirdly early. At five months pregnant, it was also starting to be fairly obvious, so I fessed up after a gig in Hyde Park and told the tour manager and everyone else that I was expecting.

That was the last gig I ever worked for that rock star. It was also the last time I ever heard from that crew. There are no contracts for crew or even session musicians. You get the gig based on someone you know who knows someone else, you shake on it and then they call you and tell you where and when to turn up, but the whole time you are instantly disposable and, at some point, for some reason, they just stop calling you. Getting pregnant was the biggest mistake I could have made as a woman who wanted to work in the music industry.

And so the die was cast, although I'm not sure I knew it. Yes, we were two self-employed creatives with no reliable income and no clue what lay in store on the other side of birth, or 'splashdown' as we had begun to call it. It's probably largely due to my privilege that I assumed our transition into parenthood would be nothing other than seamless. Motherhood was just another thing I was going to ace. I set about reading all the books and doing all the classes. I wrote a birth plan that was four pages long, colour-coded and laminated (I can only imagine how hard the midwives laughed when we were out of earshot). I truly, *truly* believed that I could control how this was going to go. I thought it would be like everything else in my life – that with the right preparation and hard work, I would have a brilliant birth, be a brilliant mum and build a brilliant life. It didn't occur to me that, from the moment I was pregnant, so much of what was going to happen was entirely out of my control.

It was the arrogance of youth, the confidence that comes with privilege. It was the ignorance of a woman who's been told one thing by society her whole life, only to discover when her legs are spread and there's five medical professionals peering into her uterus, one of whom has their arms inside her, that when it comes down to it, she has absolutely no say in how this whole thing is going to go.

All our arrogant protestations that 'a baby was going to fit in with our lives', and that 'nothing would change', suddenly glowed with ignorance and naivety. Even if I wanted to get a proper job with a proper pay cheque, I couldn't. I couldn't even figure out how to run a bath, let alone a bloody touring crew. Falling pregnant and having a baby would render *me* – not my husband – at best temporarily unemployable and at worst permanently so. Touring was out of the question – no one was going to hire a pregnant production assistant when there were plenty of other non-pregnant production assistants out there desperate for work. I needed a plan.

6

Splashdown

While I wasn't fully conscious of the discrepancies between my version of our joint circumstance versus the version my husband got to experience, there's no doubt I felt it on some level. It wasn't just the obvious, logistical issues of me finding a job with a pregnant belly on display (at first) or a baby in tow (later). There was also the subtle financial imbalance it created in our relationship.

All of a sudden, I wasn't able to reliably contribute to the family economy and, as a woman who'd always worked and paid her bills, I found that hard. I also loved to spend the money I made, so only having access to a bank account I wasn't able to pay much into because I was growing a human that we'd both chosen to have, meant neither of us really knew what an acceptable level of spending was for me.

Unusually for us, we did make attempts to sit down and talk about this. We *tried* to communicate but, it turns out, talking about money has always been (and often continues to be) our Achilles heel. We simply could not do it without an explosive argument. I don't know why we didn't recognise that we needed help with this conversation. I don't think couples' therapy was something we even knew we could have access to at this point. Instead, we just continued having exactly the same arguments around money and, by association, around the various freedoms we both felt we had or didn't have, while we carried on preparing for a baby that was coming whether we were ready or not.

Eventually, we came to a decision that neither of us were particularly happy with, but that we both recognised as our only option. Being self-employed meant there was no such thing as maternity leave for me, so Jimmy and I decided that I would stay at home with the baby and claim state maternity pay, while he would tour as hard as he could.

The idea of being a stay-at-home mum actually excited me at this point. It seemed, and I can't actually believe I'm typing this, like the easy option. How lovely, I thought, to wake up, snuggle the baby, make her organic porridge, dress her in a stylish collection of Scandi-style clothes purchased from small, independent boutiques I discovered on Instagram, pack her up in her Bugaboo and leave the house in a stylish but understated outfit that was practical for motherhood but also still pretty fucking cool, to go and have lunch with my other new-mum friends who I'd met at NCT, during which the baby would nap (of course!) and finally head home to get dinner ready, do bathtime, read a story before putting her down to sleep and settling in the living room with a glass of wine and a boxset. Sure, Jimmy would be away a lot, but it was just one small baby . . . how hard could it possibly be?

Reader, as I'm sure you know by now, it turns out it was really fucking hard and another less-than-subtle lesson in understanding that an expectation is always a resentment waiting to happen.

I went into labour on 14 November at some point in the evening, after I'd eaten a steak and jacket potato. It was the beginning of a 38-hour labour and when that was over, I genuinely thought that was the hard part done.

I'll give you a minute here to stop laughing

Yep. I was that idiot. I was the idiot who thought labour, a torn labia, seven stitches in a place where stitches should never be and a distinct memory of shitting the bed was the worst it was ever going to get. There's a picture of me, Jimmy and Billie, taken literally minutes after she was born, and while I love it because it's the first ever picture of her and of us as a family, it also gives me the heebie-jeebies because I see the shock and trauma in my face. I also feel a sharp stab of fear and a weighty sadness for Little Jimmy and Little Cat, because they had no clue, not a scooby, of the challenges that awaited them the minute they left that hospital.

I spent one night in hospital. I was on a ward and Jimmy wasn't allowed to stay with me so when he was kicked out at 8pm, I was all alone. I haven't felt that level of loneliness and fear before or since. I had just been through a 38-hour labour, I hadn't slept in two days, I'd spent the first twelve hours of labour vomiting with every contraction. Add to that, the very real physical pain I felt having just pushed something the size of a basketball out of a hole the size of a golf ball and I'm sure we can all agree, the physical and mental depletion meant I wasn't in much of a state to navigate keeping a brand-new tiny human alive.

At about 2am that morning, I couldn't get my baby to stop crying. I was panicking, and the adrenaline coursing through me was the only thing keeping me awake after nearly seventy-two hours of barely any sleep. I rushed to the midwives' station as quickly as my swollen vulva and seven stitches would allow me, and, in between exhausted sobs, I asked them what I should do.

'When was the last time you fed her?' a midwife said casually, without looking up from her computer screen.

A tidal wave of shame washed through me as I realised I probably hadn't fed her since 8pm or 9pm the night before. Here we were, five or six hours later, and I hadn't fucking fed my baby, who needed to eat pretty much all the time. How could I not have known that? I mean, I *did* know that, but somehow, when it came down to it, I hadn't been able to do even the most basic of things to keep my baby alive and healthy. I felt like a soldier who'd done all his training only to find that, when the moment came to put his head above the parapet and fire, he was frozen with fear.

I shuffled back to bed, wiping my tears away with a corner of my baby's cellular blanket, and nursed her. She drank greedily, her needs finally being met, her body occasionally shuddering with the aftershocks of crying hysterically for hours. I sobbed silently but uncontrollably. In the darkest hours of that first night, I had a lot of alone time to convince myself that I wasn't cut out for this motherhood lark, that I wasn't a natural mother, that I had made a terrible mistake. It seems dramatic, and it probably was, but I was, quite liter-ally, out of my goddam mind. I hadn't slept. I was alone. I was scared. I was pretty sure I was defective as a woman.

Those defects, which I so carefully carved into my psyche that night as truths beyond all reproach, proved to be incredibly difficult to override. They also proved to be fertile ground for the overwhelming fear to morph into red-hot anger. They were the perfect launch pad for that anger to spew forth from me frequently and project itself onto Jimmy with little to no warning. They say that hurt people hurt people and, boy, did that birth hurt me – and not just physically; it stung me on an emotional level because it made me question everything about myself and the life I'd created and the world I inhabited. I felt deeply, deeply unsafe in my new role, and like an animal cornered and frightened, I lashed out.

Breastfeeding didn't go well for me either. When it goes well, breastfeeding is one of the wonders of our world, but when it doesn't go well, it's nothing short of a violent assault on the mental health of new mums. For me, every feed was incredibly painful. If it wasn't a cracked nipple, it was a blister, or mastitis or nipple thrush. I was in hospital twice in the first eight weeks post-partum with mastitis so severe I was delusional with fever. Most of the time I fed her a 50/50 combination of breast milk and blood. Whenever Billie woke from a nap, I would physically shake because I knew I'd have to feed her. I would feed her and notice my own tears splashing onto her cheek. It was a devastatingly difficult period of time for me, when I was at my most vulnerable.

I was also, of course, hyper-aware of the 'breast is best' ethos that was being pushed down every new mother's throat at the time. The propaganda that came from the mouths of every NCT teacher, midwife and health visitor made you feel like giving formula to your baby was akin to giving it a mixture of tequila, cocaine and dung beetles. Despite everyone's gentle suggestions that I supplement with formula, I was resolute that breastfeeding was the one 'natural' element of motherhood that I was going to get right.

Eventually, after nine weeks, I was nursing Billie and squeezing my mum's hand so tightly because of the pain, that she was wincing.

'You can't carry on like this, darling,' she said. 'It's not okay. I know you want to breastfeed, but the cost for doing it can't be your mental health. I've kept my mouth shut until now, but I'm going to buy some formula and a bottle and I think you should try it.'

I was devastated. I didn't receive this in the way it was intended, which was with kindness and concern. I received it as further proof that I was a shit mum, but I didn't stop her when she put her coat on and went to the shops. I didn't stop her when she made the bottle and carefully, without a word, put it in the arm of the sofa next to me. When she suggested I give it a go, I didn't stop myself picking up the bottle and putting it to the lips of my baby. What I *did* do, however, was make Jimmy hold the bottle too, so that he couldn't, at a later date, blame me for breaking Billie. That's how insane I was at the time.

Of course, delighted by the blood-free sustenance she was finally receiving, Billie glugged that bottle down like a prop-forward with a yard of ale at a rugby husting. I should have felt relief, but I didn't. I felt hurt. She liked the formula – that poisonous, synthetic, Big Pharma money-making stuff – more than my milk. Of course she did – I was a shit mum and I had nothing to offer but shit breast milk.

The next morning, after Billie had slept through for the first time on a full tummy, I called the health visitor. I was hysterical. I could barely get the words out but I managed to say, 'I've just given her a bottle of formula and I need you to tell me I'm not a terrible mum.' What the health visitor said next was, without doubt, the most traumatic thing anyone has said to me, before or since.

'Well, lovey,' she started sympathetically, 'don't worry. You can always try to undo the damage you've done when it comes to weaning.'

The. Damage. You've. Done.

To the health visitor, maybe it was a flippant comment, a thoughtless one. Maybe she didn't even really know what she'd said. To me, though, it was a dagger through the final vestiges of hope that I could, actually, be a good mother. As she said, the damage had been done. There was no fixing it. There was only the potential mitigation of it later down the line. I had done what I always feared I would do – cause serious harm to my baby. The wound caused by those words would remain open and pus-filled, riddled with infection, for many, many years to come. Even today, as I write this, I feel a stab of shame and humiliation for not being better and doing better as a mother. I still, even now, can't quite shed the belief that I am, at my core, a bad mum.

Jimmy was home for a month after Billie was born, which was longer than most men got at the time in terms of paternal leave. In early January, though, Jimmy left to go on tour for seven months. He came home every two or three weeks, but it was always temporary. It was also essential – we needed the money – and although I understood that, I also hated him for leaving me, for leaving us. Through the anger and resentment (that I knew wasn't reasonable but there nonetheless), I didn't consider that he might hate leaving too. I didn't consider that he worried about us every minute he was away. I didn't know that he knew I wasn't okay but also didn't know how to get beyond my veneer of 'coping' without setting off the defensive beast in me, a beast that was so sensitive to the idea that anyone would dare to question my capabilities as a mother that it would rip you limb from limb if you dared to try.

While Jimmy was away, I was in charge. While I hated being alone, there was part of me that knew some things were easier when he was gone. When I was on my own, it was my way or the highway. I didn't have to clear anything with another adult or worry about anyone else's feelings or schedules. I could run the show however I liked, and even if logistically and physically it was pretty relentless, mentally the load was easier to manage when I only had myself to clean up after and consult about the day-to-day running of our lives. Then Jimmy would come back and that routine would be blown up immediately with the thud of his suitcase landing in the hall.

I will live and die by the idea that two things can be true at the same time. I was always overwhelmed with joy to have Jimmy home and, at the same time, immediately irritated that he was there barging his way back into a life that wasn't the same as when he'd left it. A lot of people assume that when you're in a relationship with someone who works away a lot that it's the time apart that's hard. It isn't. It's the transitions. It's the few days before he leaves and the few days after he comes back. Those are the pain points.

During this time, I appeared to be coping but, behind the scenes, I really wasn't. Postnatal depression had taken me in its grip – and I had no idea. Yes, I cried a lot. Yes, I spent a worrying amount of time convincing myself that everyone would be happier without me. Yes, I knew I would jump in front of a bus for Billie, but, dig as deep as I could, I still couldn't identify a feeling I recognised as love for her. I was numb to all meaningful connection – all interactions were a monumental effort – but I thought that was normal when you have a newborn. I was sleep-deprived, on my feet all day, I had no time for myself . . . of course I was going to feel a bit down and disconnected, right?

Jimmy tried to help in the best way he knew how. When he came home, he would whisk the baby away, and on the one hand, that's what I needed. After weeks of solo parenting, I didn't want to be near anyone. I wanted to be left alone; I didn't want to be touched or spoken to. I didn't want to have to change a nappy or have a bath with a baby in a rocker next to me. I didn't want to spend my days talking to a baby who never had anything interesting to say, and so, when Jimmy came home and took over, part of me was overcome with relief.

But it also meant that my isolation was complete. I was alone, completely and entirely. It took me years to realise that being left alone during that time wasn't what I needed. What I needed was to be looked after. I didn't understand that, I didn't know how to ask for that and I was even less comfortable with the reality of being someone who *needed* that. I come from a 'pull yourself together' family, and while that has served me well on occasions, it was my downfall here. I felt overwhelmed and suffocated by the relentless responsibility of parenting when Jimmy wasn't home and untethered to anyone when he was. I was grateful that he was doing bedtime and bathtime and that I could leave the house without a baby, a buggy and a bag, but I also felt so desperately unconnected and acutely alone that my anger and resentment only grew. I wanted space but I also wanted to be held . . . I just didn't know that.

My birth story may not seem like it fits seamlessly into a book about the mental load, but it was the moment I realised that my responsibilities within our new family set-up had increased exponentially. It wasn't that Jimmy's responsibilities hadn't increased as well – of course they had, and I was aware of that at the time – but he didn't have boobs to feed her with, he hadn't been physically attached to her in a way that meant she needed him on a cellular level. He could work away from home for weeks at a time; he could decide he wanted a shower, and have a shower. In the early days, it felt like I needed a spreadsheet to manage the logistics of taking a shower.

None of what happened during that first year was healthy or conscious and we were both doing the best we could with the information we had, but when, four years later, I sat Jimmy down and told him we were separating, I had no idea that the seeds for that conversation had been sown in the first year of being a mother. It would take hours and hours and thousands of pounds' worth of couples' therapy for us to figure that out, when we needed to come together the most, we had inadvertently and unknowingly severed everything that had held us together, and honestly, there wasn't that much to start with.

Looking back, I think it was nothing more than stubbornness that kept us together. Perhaps it was also a lack of energy and mental bandwidth to even consider the upheaval that a separation or divorce would have required. Whatever it was, we survived what we both accept now as the hardest year of our lives and although things did get easier, and we found our feet, what came next – me going back to work, us having another baby, buying a house and everything else in between – was built on foundations that were terminally cracked.

7

Bringing Home the Bacon
(and Cooking it Too)

'*After a child is born the lives of its mother and father diverge,
so that where before they were living in a state of some equality,
now they exist in a sort of feudal relation to each other.*' – *A
Life's Work*, Rachel Cusk

As a new mum, I learned early on that the biggest lie of all
was that we could have it all. Or, perhaps more accurately,
that having it all was one thing; *doing* it all was something
entirely different. In my early days as a new mum, I was
broken under the pressure of all the expectations I perceived
were placed upon me. I so desperately wanted my version of
motherhood to look as effortless as everyone else's seemed to,
but instead, I was floundering and gasping for air.

It didn't take long for me to realise that I'd been conned.
Motherhood is instinctive, they'd say. It's the most natural
thing in the world, but also, you should really buy all these
baby books telling you how to do it because you actually
don't know much about anything to do with rearing a baby
and even though those books all say different things, don't,
whatever you do, bring that up in any kind of social setting

with other new parents because you'll upset everyone simultaneously.

Be sure to look after yourself. Put your oxygen mask on first, but also don't be selfish. Mastitis is uncomfortable, sure, but breast is best, so just keep going. It's what good mums do. Feeling down? Oh, it's just the baby blues; it'll pass. But it is a bit messy in here. Are you coping okay? Because if not, we can give you some meds, but don't take them if you're breastfeeding, which, of course, you *should* do because, did I mention, breast is best? Oh and make sure you find some time for yourself, but not too much time, because babies need to feel attached. What? You have to go back to work? Oh dear. Tsk tsk tsk. Well, what on earth are you going to do with the baby? No one asked your husband that? Well, of course they didn't. No, I don't know why. Best not to over-think it, lovey. Also, you can have it all now, you know . . . as long as you don't expect 'having it all' to mean good mental health, a chance at any real career progression, a feeling of calm, peace and fulfilment, or a conscience clear of mum-guilt.

It's not easy for me to write this, but the first year of my eldest daughter's life was the worst of mine. From the moment she arrived earthside the Newborn baby version of the mental load (arguably the most intensive of all the versions of the mental load) was louder than a Taylor Swift concert. But instead of them all singing the same song at once, the voices in my head all sang different songs at the same time. Things I wanted to say but couldn't, because I knew everyone would stare at me like I was a mad woman, swirled around the constant ticker tape of tasks that needed doing. No matter how many tasks I completed, there were always more to fill the gaps. Crossing off items on my to-do list simply made room for more 'to-dos', and while I tried to look like a normal mum and carry on doing the hardest thing I'd ever done – looking after a newborn – I lived in a constant state of fight or flight. I wanted to cry and scream and ask for help but I also, desperately, didn't want to do any of those things, because that's not what good mothers did. It's not what good women, who weren't defective in some way, did. I had to pretend like I wasn't broken somehow, like I had it all under control.

This, then, is where I was mentally when it was time for me to step out of the newborn bubble and start living real life as a wife and mother. I was totally unmoored from any sense of self. I felt as if I was outside of my body, pushing it where it needed to go, moving it when it needed to be moved, nodding or shaking its head at the appropriate times. There was no part of me that believed I could do this, but every part of me knew I had to anyway. I knew I had to wake up every day and commit to doing the one thing I was really bad at – mothering.

I'd go through the motions of waking up Billie, getting her dressed and fed. I'd turn over the laundry. I'd clean the house. I'd try to play with Billie, but the feeling that there were *so many other things* that needed doing would gnaw away at any attempts I made to play tea parties. All I ever wanted to do in that first year or two, if I'm honest, is crawl into my bed, pull the covers over my head and leave the world. Was I suicidal? I don't think so. I don't think I ever thought about killing myself in a practical sense, but I definitely fantasised about how I could just absent myself from the world. It's a subtle distinction but there was no desire on my part to harm myself. Instead, I just wished there was a 'World' switch that I could just move to 'Off'.

When Billie was about three months old, I managed to get myself a job. It had become clear pretty quickly that, with my current mental state, the isolation I felt being a stay-at-home mum wasn't good for me and so, through a friend of a friend, I'd found a job managing a charity that the director ran from her mansion in Henley. While it wasn't strictly within the music industry, a large part of my job was organising a huge rock music show that we held at the Royal Albert Hall each year to raise funds. I was very good friends with her daughter, who had also had a baby a few months before me. The director was more than happy for me to bring Billie with me and even offered to organise a nanny share. I'd done the impossible. I'd found a job with a newborn that remarkably came with childcare. Once again, Jimmy shook his head, smiled and asked me how I always managed to land on my feet.

From then on, I was a working mum, and most of the time I was on my own because Jimmy was away so much. Having a job was great for the part of me that still existed from my life before Billie, but looking back, doing it with a baby while my husband was away all the time was too much for me. I would wake up, fuzzy-headed and tired at about 6am. Billie would wake up at 7am (God bless that child for sleeping through the night early on) and I'd get her dressed and fed. I'd turn the laundry over. Clean the house. Pack my work bag. Pack Billie's bag. I'd drive to work and spend the day working, all the while keeping an ear out for Billie to make sure she was okay with the nanny. If the nanny wasn't there, I'd juggle. Then I'd drive home, feed Billie, cook dinner for myself, bathe her, read her a story and pop her into bed. After that, I'd open a bottle of wine and start cleaning and preparing for the next day.

Against the backdrop of the daily routine was the constant management of schedules, appointments, nursery application forms, bed changes, car services, bin days, trying to keep up with friends and family and all the other grim minutiae that lodges itself in our brains. I knew I was tired and burning out, but I had no idea how much of a toll *doing* it all was taking on my soul. Rather than think about it, I'd open another bottle of wine and drown the fear under three, four or five glasses of Malbec every night. There was no room or space to breathe, but rather than speak up and ask for help, I just kept going. The shame of not being able to do this whole working mum thing was one failure too many and I wasn't going to fuck this up too. I was literally bringing the bacon home *and* cooking it and cleaning up afterwards.

Our generation is not the first to struggle with the pressures of being a working mum. In 1983 – which is, God help us, already over forty years ago – sociologist Arlie Russell Hochschild suggested in her book *The Second Shift* that there was a tension, or as she called it, 'the stalled revolution', between women's changing perceptions of their role in relationships and the workplace versus the world's resistance to accommodate these changes. Basically, marriages were falling apart quicker than cheap slime because women were starting to admit and/or realise that they'd been given the rough end of the marital and social pineapple. When their partners didn't co-sign on this forward-thinking, 'new way' of living, resentments set in quickly and divorce lawyers were left counting their piles of money from second homes in sunny Spain.

Hochschild's book is one of the seminal texts on the labour divide in relationships, but even her approach is limited. In 1983, she focused solely on working mothers versus non-working mothers and how our audacious infiltration of the workplace affected our marriages. I'm not sure even Hochschild had fully understood the mental virus that would continue to ravage not just marriages, but women's mental health, their pay packet, their ability to progress at work and, perhaps most terrifyingly, their freedom of choice. Or maybe she did; she just didn't want to scare the shit out of us.

The concept of the mental load emerged in the 80s and it's no surprise that it happened in that decade. Think Melanie Griffith in *Working Girl*, Dolly Parton in *Nine to Five* and Goldie Hawn in *Private Benjamin*. The 80s was a decade when society began to tell us that this wasn't, in fact, a man's world, and that sisters were doing it for themselves. Great. Feminism. Tick! The problem is that we were still also doing it for everyone else. *But*, they hollered, *you wanted to have it all . . . Here it is!* A response loaded with the same tones of a parent telling a teenager that, sure, they can take up an extra-curricular activity, *as long as your grades don't start to slip.* For women, a job outside the home was the equivalent to the extra-curricular activity, and we were only going to be allowed to do that if our 'grades' – a clean house, child-care, dinner on the table – were not affected as a result. Of course, no one bothered to ask women if we wanted it all to begin with or if we just wanted some fucking help with the laundry and kids.

But what did we know? We'd never played the game before. We didn't know the rules. We didn't realise there *were* rules. We thought we'd cleverly won our right to equality, that we'd managed to get one over the men, when, in reality, they were the ones who'd hoodwinked us into socialised slavery. Unpaid labour, the mental load, became the shackles around our ankles with chains just long enough to let us go to the office, but always firmly rooted in the home.

None of this is to undermine the work that the second wave of feminism did for women's rights. Those powerhouses managed to dismantle a behemothic, centuries-old social structure that most women hadn't even realised was there at all. In my opinion, no generation of women has done more for women's rights, despite it being deeply flawed in its exclusive focus on white middle- and upper-class women. The absence of working-class women and women of colour, and the lack of intersectionality in the movement meant that, while it laid foundations, it failed to look back, reach out a hand and drag *all* women along with it, the legacy of which is still woefully apparent today.

While there are lots of things that people can point to in order to show us that equality is a job done – *you've got the vote, you can work, you can get a mortgage, you're not legally allowed to be fired for being pregnant* – we are still a long way from being on an equal footing. Those high-ticket items may look like equality, but it's the invisible stuff that, no matter how hard we try to shine a light on it, people who don't want to look at it can easily deny the existence of.

And that's the mental load. As Hochschild says, it's the invisible, unpaid labour of running a household that defaults to women as opposed to the 'smooth choicelessness' of men, who never have to spend a minute wondering how they're going to go back to work after having a baby. But it's become more than that. It's no longer just the logistical burden of running a household that women tend to bear. The mental load has followed us, sneakily, into the workplace, too. Women are more likely to take on what's referred to as 'non-promotable tasks' at work – tasks that aren't paid and offer little value when it comes to workplace advancement. These are things like organising work social events, collecting money for birthdays, births or deaths, cleaning up meeting rooms, making coffee, taking notes, providing emotional support for colleagues (this also applies to being the go-to emotional support in the home too) and welcoming or mentoring new employees.

The same patterns happen when your kids start school, too. Unless you actively request otherwise, the mum's number will always be the first contact listed, meaning you're the one who will get all the phone calls, emails and text messages. If you've got a child at school, you'll know the volume of contact from primary school, especially, can be overwhelming. No one ever asked Jimmy if he wanted to be on the class WhatsApp group; all requests came to me. It took me one term to realise that the class WhatsApp was never going to bring out anything but the worst in me and so Jimmy – who is inherently a better human than I am – took one for the Sims team there and it's been his responsibility ever since. Also, it's worth asking yourself, how many dads are there on your school PTA? I'm willing to bet that there aren't many.

The fact is, the current displacement of the mental load isn't about keeping women 'in their place'. In reality, it's one of the most effective tools society has of tricking women into thinking they can go wherever they want to go in society . . . as long as where they want to go is not over the heads of their male counterparts. It's the perfect 'you've made your bed and now you have to lie in it' gaslight and the irony that we made *all the fucking beds* appears lost on everyone. Yes, we wanted to bring home the bacon, but we didn't realise we'd be the only ones cooking it and cleaning up afterwards. Or, perhaps we did, we just thought it would be okay, we could handle it, what could possibly go wrong?

The reality of being a working mum is one that only those who have done it can even begin to understand, and I don't include myself in that. I haven't done it, not properly at least. I was always self-employed, so while the security of a pay cheque was something I craved, I was always grateful I didn't have to figure out a way to defy space and time so that I could be in the boardroom and at nursery pick-up at the same time. I was poor but available. I wasn't sure I could pay the mortgage but I also didn't have to pay nursery fees and, honestly, if I had to do it all over again, I think I'd still pick 'poor but available' over 'manipulate the space-time continuum'. For those of you reading this who did just that for years and years, I salute you. I see you and I stand in your honour because I have no fucking idea how you did it, and, just in case no one has ever told you this: you're incredible. Truly.

I spent the first two or three years as a mum torn between really believing in the concept of, and wanting to be, the perfect wife and mother. After all, that's what I'd seen growing up. Happy marriages were made up of characters that played their roles well and, never one to do anything half-assed, I was going to win the fucking Oscar for Lead Actress in the maternal, sexy, houseproud, successful, funny, put-together, strong category. But, while I cleaned the floorboards as I trod them, core resentments sprouted from the deepest, darkest corners of my gut and flowed like pus into my brain, infecting everything they touched. Eventually, these resentments became impossible to ignore and while I looked at my marriage and the way it made me feel, I was looking up the number for one of those divorce lawyers, sunning themselves on the Costa Brava, because *I was done*; this was not what love was supposed to look like or feel like.

8

The Disney Dad and the Evil (Step)Mum

'For the strength of the pack is the Wolf, and the Wolf is the strength of the pack.' – Mowgli, *The Jungle Book*

I don't know if I've mentioned it (sarcasm noted), but during the first year of my eldest's life, Jimmy ended up being on tour for seven months. He would be home every two or three weeks, for a few days, and then leave again. I was always torn between desperately wanting him to come home and not wanting him to fuck up the rhythm and routine I'd managed to implement.

It's a strange thing when you have a partner who's away a lot – especially when you have a baby or a young child in the mix. When they're gone, you wish they were home, and when they're home you can't wait for them to leave again. There's no baseline. You live an existence of extremes.

The minute they walk back through the door, you're elated. You feel like you can breathe again, take a shower without listening for a wail or a scream and not have to cook every goddamn meal. It's instant relief. Your expectations are high (there's that word again). Your partner is back, your teammate, your ride or die. Now, you think, you'll only have to do half the work because your other half will pick up . . . well, the other half. But, as I've said before: *an expectation is a resentment waiting to happen*, and it doesn't take long until you realise that rather than reducing your workload, they've actually just increased it by 100 per cent.

Ten minutes later, you're frustrated, managing a low-level rage, because they don't know what's going on, how things work, what the schedule is and they have the audacity to act like they live there! Their suitcase explodes, the dirty laundry lands in the basket, increasing the pile tenfold, and yet there doesn't seem to be any impetus to put any of the dirty clothes *in* the washing machine. They're just abandoned for the laundry fairies – and not even sorted into lights and darks. FML. The silent message is clear: *Here's some more laundry for you!* Before I know it, I'm fantasising about how to stab him in his sleep and get away with it, but I won't need to, I think! There isn't a judge in the land who would blame me for taking this selfish, thoughtless, obnoxious piece of shit out of this world.

The house that, just ten minutes ago, was clean, calm and organised, is now vibrating with chaos and noise. It feels suddenly cramped, and a feeling of claustrophobia starts to creep up on you. The control freak in me bursts forth and I start spouting things like, 'No, that's not how we do it,' or, 'Actually can you just leave that where it is?' or, 'We've actually got a whole routine that works really well, so can you let me do it?' All of this, every single second of it, is done against the backdrop of your baby or small child grinning and screaming because they're so delighted to see your partner (that you can't help but hate on a visceral level) that they're practically shitting themselves.

Of course, because you're not a monster, you don't want to deny them the joy of reuniting with their other parent, but at the same time, you're murderous and, perhaps, if you're willing to admit it, a little fucking jealous, not of your child, but of the feelings they get to have. The pure, unadulterated joy at seeing the other human that made them, that is genetically half of them, is an anathema to the pure, unadulterated disappointment you feel. You yearn for the ignorance of a toddler brain, the simplicity of their emotions. They don't give a shit that they've come with a mountain of laundry, they just want to cuddle their parent.

By this point, I didn't even want Jimmy to look at me. I just wanted to hand everything over to him and walk away and often, in the first year, that's what happened. He knew I was struggling, and he believed it was all about the baby. I think I believed that too. Again, to reiterate, the concept of the mental load wasn't something we'd ever heard of, so when Jimmy came home and took the baby, I think we both thought that was the rest I needed. But it wasn't. It wasn't even close, and neither of us could understand why I was still frazzled and stressed and angry and resentful.

Of course, with two free hands, I suddenly jumped into action. All those things I hadn't been able to do while solo parenting became my priority. I ran myself ragged working, cleaning, exercising, seeing friends and doing boring things like going to the dentist or getting my hair done. During this time, I'd barely see Jimmy or the baby, and while I enjoyed the freedom, there was also part of me that felt lonely, or perhaps not lonely, but isolated. There was definitely part of me that felt sad, and probably jealous that Jimmy was so focused on looking after the baby and making sure her needs were taken care of that he didn't realise I needed taking care of too.

Whenever I talk about feeling jealous of my baby in relation to my husband's relationship with her during the first year, the reaction is mixed, but fuck it. This book has to be as honest as possible if I want it to be as comforting as possible for other mothers. I *was* jealous. I'm not proud of the fact, but while I was struggling with a newborn, I had undiagnosed post-partum depression and a husband that worked away a lot. I wanted him to look after me like he looked after her. I wanted him to 'just know' (there's that reliance on telepathy again) that I was really, really struggling, and when he didn't, when he (quite rightly) focused on our baby, I hated him for it.

Of course, at no point did I actually say this out loud and, to give me some credit, there was no way I could have. I didn't know what the fuck was going on with me, and so the thought of beating myself up for not articulating it seems pointless. We were in the deepest, darkest depths of the unknown. We were a young, married couple with a baby between us, emotionally cock-blocking us every step of the way. We did the best we could, but I'm okay admitting that it wasn't really good enough, especially in terms of our relationship.

I don't want you to think, however, that I was sat in a soggy puddle of depression-induced tears while Jimmy ignored me. That's not how it went. I wasn't just unable to communicate my feelings and state of mind verbally. I also did a really good job of hiding any behaviour that might indicate I wasn't feeling tip-top, too. I went about my days looking, for all intents and purposes, like I wasn't completely unhinged.

I lived in a universe constructed entirely by me and my rules, in which I was the sun that gave life and light to everything. In contrast, Jimmy was a slightly smelly, gaseous, orbiting planet, that didn't appear to add much value to anything, apart from the occasional moment when he'd totally eclipse me, by turning up with a McDonald's or announcing that we were all going to go swimming when I'd already said no. He'd constantly put forth ideas of 'family activities' that we could all do together and when I suggested he and Billie did it without me, he'd look hurt and disappointed that I was *yet again* avoiding family time. It was never that I was *avoiding* family time, though. It was just that I felt I might physically and mentally crack, straight down the middle, if I had to spend one more minute being responsible for anyone else.

This dynamic is so common in so many households, and I like to call it Disney Dad versus the Wicked (Step)Mum. I can only talk about this in relation to having a husband who would work away for long periods of time, but I imagine it's the same for those families who only see Daddy at dinner time after he's had a long day at work. The stay-at-home parent is tired and running low on fucks. The 'just-arrived-home' parent is a novelty, something to be played with, and because time with the kids is often scarce for the parent who's absent a lot, they are reluctant to spend that time having the 'time-for-bed' fight or the homework fight or any other fight similar to the ones the 'stay-at-home' parent will have battled all day.

And, I get it. It makes sense. In 2016, our second daughter Bo arrived, and here's the good news: my second birth healed a lot of the damage from the first. I approached the whole thing differently. Despite dismissing hypnobirthing as being a bit 'vagina-whispery' for me, I did it anyway because my friend was a hypnobirthing teacher and I was just about self-aware enough to realise that doing it my way the first time definitely didn't work, so why not try something different.

I don't remember much of what happened in those classes, if I'm honest, but I do remember one thing that the teacher said that totally transformed my approach to giving birth.

'Your uterus is a muscle,' she explained, 'and all muscles need oxygen-rich blood to function at their best.'

That made sense to me. I'd been an athlete as a kid, so the physiology of muscles and the vascular system was something I understood.

'If you panic during labour,' she continued, 'you'll start producing adrenaline, and all that oxygen-rich blood will be sent to your brain and limbs for your fight-or-flight response. Your uterus will have to finish what it's started but it'll be doing it on limited resources, making it longer, harder and more painful.'

What. The. Actual. Fuck. My head literally exploded. It was a lightning-bolt moment. It was practically a spiritual experience. It suddenly all made sense. I shoved my hand in the air.

'Sorry,' I stammered, almost unable to speak while my brain was shattering with this new knowledge, 'just to be clear . . .

you're saying that all I have to do is stay calm and birth will be, if not easy, then not traumatic?'

'Yep, that's it.'

When I went into labour with Bo, it was 9.30am on 30 August 2016. I put my headphones on immediately. I lay down on the sofa and I started listening to affirmations and playlists I'd set up ahead of time. I spoke to no one. I focused on my breathing. I visualised sending all that oxygen-filled blood to my uterus and I shut the outside world off. Meanwhile, Jimmy ran around filling up the birthing pool and letting the midwife know what was going on. By 12.30pm, Bo had arrived, almost en caul and in such a state of calm that the midwife had to cut the umbilical cord earlier than I would have liked to make sure she was okay. She was.

The trauma of my first birth was never acknowledged, let alone managed, and it continued to spill out sideways through the first year of Billie's life. It caused me, my husband, our relationship and, to some extent, our daughter, so much emotional pain for the simple fact that no one, not one person, said to me, 'You've been through a trauma and you need to heal.' Instead, I was sent home with a baby, no instructions, and a healthy dose of what I now truly believe was PTSD. But, with Bo, I was able to breastfeed without developing one blister or cracked nipple for just over a year. Nothing had changed, other than my birthing experience. I certainly wasn't a better mother and Bo wasn't a better baby. In many ways, my confidence in myself as a mum was still at an all-time low, but my second birthing experience was the first step on my way to understanding the trauma I'd experienced the first time. The connection, in my opinion, between a calm birth and a subsequently positive newborn experience cannot be denied.

Despite my positive experience birthing Bo, the result was that I was left with a toddler and a newborn to be responsible for. Jimmy was still away a lot and we continued to struggle with how to manage the dynamic when he was home. He didn't want to walk through the front door and find himself emerging from a tunnel into the domestic colosseum where a fight to the death is in full swing. He wanted to put his suitcase down, have a cup of tea, unpack and put his slippers on. It used to infuriate me that he expected to be able to do this before getting stuck in. I never experienced the luxury of getting myself sorted while someone else held the baby, and no matter how deep I dug, I couldn't find it within myself to give that luxury to him the minute he walked through the door. I felt like he was taking everything for granted and all I wanted was to be tagged out for the first time in three weeks. I was sick of hearing my own voice, I was sick of having the same fight with a toddler who didn't want to eat what I'd cooked. I was touched out* and done in. Why couldn't he see that?

Of course, the real question is: *Why does it always have to be a battle?* The answer is simple: because we didn't tell each other how we were feeling and we had no idea how to ask

---

* Touched out is when, as a mother, you have become overstimulated due to too much physical touch from a significant other or a child (mostly a child!) and wish to limit the frequency of people's physical contact with your body. Author's note: this also applies to dogs and cats who feel entitled to sit on you when you've finally got the kids to sleep and you've sat down to watch *The Real Housewives of* Wherever.

for what we needed. I don't think we could have even *identified* what we were feeling or what we needed. Those early years are relentless and there's almost no time to reflect. We were fire-fighting and we just knew that everything felt wrong and itchy and out of control.

And while all of this may seem fairly obvious, what's less obvious is the effect that this Disney Dad vs. Evil (Step)Mum dynamic can have on the relationship between yourself and your partner. In my experience, I know how easy it is to be so focused on the kids and their behaviour and their *stuff* that you almost forget you're in a romantic relationship with someone who is supposed to be your best friend, your one person in this world. Add to that the resentments that grow because you always feel like you're the bad cop or because you constantly feel that the minute you walk in the house someone is there, behind the door, waiting to nag or criticise or both.

I wish I'd known that we didn't have to be on different teams in those early years. I wish we'd been able to see beyond the constant comparisons about who was more tired, or who worked harder, or who earned more money. I wish he'd been able to see the invisible labour I did and I wish I'd been able to empathise with the pressure he felt as the breadwinner. I wish we'd been able to see that *we* – Jimmy and I – were at the top of the family tree and the kids came in below us. I wish we'd not put the kids on a rickety pedestal while we staggered around beneath arguing about whose responsibility it was to catch them when they fell.

I wish we'd not forgotten that we chose each other once, that there was a time when we were delighted to see each other walk in through the front door. I wish we'd not disconnected so completely. I wish we'd realised that the way to succeed was to not allow ourselves to be divided and conquered.

I wish we'd protected the parental team like our lives depended on it – because honestly, they sort of did. I know now that the vibe between Jimmy and I needs to be one of 'no man left behind', of 'no matter what', of 'I've got you'. In the face of those things that kids do that we allow to come between us as adults – the tantrums, the screaming, the fighting, the mess, the tears – we need solid and unbreakable defences, even if that looks like:

- 'Not now. I'm catching up with Mummy/Daddy about their day.'
- Hiding in a room together with the door closed
- 'Don't talk to Mummy/Daddy like that. They're my best friend.'
- 'No, I'm not reading you a story until I've had a chance to give my best friend a cuddle and ask him/her how his/her day was.'

Or something like that. I think what I'd love to achieve between me and Jimmy is less a Disney Dad vs. Evil (Step) Mum vibe and more a Katniss and Peeta against two tiny citizens of the Capitol.

And, yes, I love *The Hunger Games*.

9

Keeping My Side of the Street Clean

'The universe is seeming really huge right now. I need
something to hold on to.' – *We Were Liars*, E. Lockhart

I have never understood the difference between *fault* and
responsibility, but I've come to learn that it's a question of
perspective. I would always come at a problem or a conflict
with the sole intention of identifying who is to blame or
who's at fault and, surprise, surprise, it was never me! There's
a saying that I try to remind myself of when I start muttering
under my breath about something Jimmy has or hasn't done,
and it's this: *Focus on keeping your side of the street clean.* Back
in the day, I was obsessed with assessing Jimmy's side of the
street and how clean or dirty it was. I would spend my life
looking over at his side, pointing out all the shit that was
wrong with it. Maybe his clothes were all over the floor, or
he'd come back late from work and not called, or he'd not
thought to wipe his skid marks off the toilet, or he'd forgotten
an anniversary. It didn't matter that I was occasionally guilty
of those things too, or similar infractions – I was always on
high-alert for proof that a) he was a crappy husband and b)

he didn't really love me. No matter how often I tried this approach, and no matter how many times it ended in disaster, it didn't occur to me to try something new and start focusing on keeping my side of the street clean.

Any argument between Jimmy and I was a wrangle to see which one of us could find the other guilty and lock them in the metaphorical stocks. But when either of us was released from the stocks, nothing had really changed. A relationship can't be maintained if you spend all your energy with your back to the wall, keeping your partner in your sights, doing all you can to avoid the humiliation of those stocks. This is especially true in a marriage, and trust me, I spent many years testing this theory.

The early years of my marriage were an exercise in dodging blame, in defending myself to the death, in doing all I could do to not be 'found out' or confirmed as wrong. Defensive was my middle name. I can count on one hand the times I said sorry and I know exactly how many times I was the *first one* to say sorry: none. Not one. I did things to 'test' him, knowing he'd fail.

I once left a pile of his clothes on the stairs and decided to see how long it would take for him to pick it up and take it upstairs. By the third week, I was so self-righteous in my silent rage that it ended up in a blazing row that we took weeks to recover from. At the time I thought I was a genius. I'd proven a point and nothing he could say or do could justify his complete lack of awareness when it came to the mental load. All I'd really done is humiliate him and make it clear that we were not on the same team. I tried to feel superior but, really, I felt like shit. It had been an exercise, once again, in focusing on Jimmy's side of the street and the things *he* wasn't picking up.

There was method in my madness. On reflection, I think I saw my 'stair pile' as a mini strike. I'd read about the women of Iceland and how, on 24 October 1975, they had gone on a national strike. Almost fifty years ago, the Icelandic women were clear on the things we are still struggling to understand in our own society today – that women were undervalued and underappreciated. They knew there was only one way to prove this to a patriarchal society that didn't care to listen and that was by downing tools. While the strike was primarily about protesting 'wage discrepancy and unfair employment practices',[1] it was also about demonstrating 'the indispensable work of women for Iceland's economy and society'[2] and highlighting the extent of the *unpaid* labour that women took responsibility for every day – a responsibility that men failed to recognise the importance of. It was about shoving the reality of the mental load in the face of men who did half as much and earned twice more.

Billed as *Women's Day Off*, the strike was led by women's organisations who encouraged all Icelandic women to not do their paid jobs and also do no housework or child rearing. Ninety per cent of Icelandic women participated in the strike and, I'm sure it'll come as no surprise to you, the country disintegrated into chaos. Less than a year later, the Icelandic government passed a law guaranteeing equal rights to men and women.

Out of a population of 220,000, there gathered a crowd of 25,000 women in the centre of Reykjavik. There were speeches, singing and celebrations while employers stocked up on sweets, pencils and paper to help entertain the children in the workplace while their fathers tried to juggle their jobs and childcare. I think my favourite fact regarding the Icelandic women's strike is that, on that day, sausages sold out across the country. Of course they did – what's easier to cook than a sausage? A fish finger, perhaps? But that was a no-go, because the fish factories closed that day due to the fact that the majority of factory workers were women.

The impact was swift and severe. The day of the strike became known colloquially as 'the long Friday', although I'm sure there were men who had other, less polite ways to describe it. Not only did it lead to Parliament passing a law protecting gender equality, it also paved the way for the very first female president *globally* to take office five years later in 1980.

However, while the women's strike in Iceland was the first of its kind on a national scale, it wasn't the first time women had gone on strike on the issue of unequal pay. In 1968, 187 women went on strike at the Ford factory in Dagenham in the UK after they were regraded as 'C' workers, meaning they were paid 15 per cent less than men who did the same job. As sewing machinists, they believed they should have been graded as 'B' workers due to their specialised skill set. I couldn't agree more. If you've ever tried to use a sewing machine, you'll know that it requires a surgical level of skill and precision, and this is coming from someone who managed to sew through their own finger in a home economics class once, so I know what I'm talking about.

The Dagenham women's strike lasted three weeks, at which point Barbara Castle, the Secretary of State for Employment and Productivity at the time, intervened. She raised the wages to 92 per cent of the men's and promised them a 'B' grade categorisation the following year. Two years later, the government passed the Equal Pay Act, which came into force in 1975. It was part of the reason the United Nations decided to name 1975 International Women's Year, hence why the women of Iceland chose to strike that same year.

There was also the Women's Strike for Equality that occurred in the USA in 1970. Like the Icelandic strike, it attempted to be a national shutdown strike that fought for issues such as free abortion on demand, equal opportunity in the workforce, free childcare, political rights for women, and social equality in relationships. While it was disruptive, it didn't have the same impact as the Icelandic strike with only 50,000 women taking part, and when President Richard Nixon vetoed a childcare bill a year later, momentum was lost.

The comforting thing that I think we can all take away from this is that the mental load, and the consequences of bearing it, is not a new issue. This is not a modern problem. We are not, as a generation, more hard-done-by, and I think it's important to understand that. If anything, our lives are almost certainly considerably easier than they were for previous generations of women. That's not to say that we shouldn't be working hard to redress the balance of the mental load, but it is worth remembering that we are not fighting this battle alone and our privilege is that we get to stand on the shoulders of women who blazed the trail.

In contrast, my strike with the pile of clothes on the stairs didn't work because no one knew I was doing it. Iceland's strike was so effective because everyone knew it was happening, the men had time to prepare and still, *still*, the country all but came to a standstill. What I thought was a valid act of defiance had ended up being an act of unkindness, designed to make Jimmy feel like a dick. It didn't empower me or make a point; it simply made me look like a bit of a bitch.

I also had to ask myself some pretty uncomfortable questions about why it's only me that suffers when I stop doing all the things, because honestly, the rest of my family don't care. They aren't remotely bothered if the dishes pile up or the floor is filthy. Why is that? Why is it that they don't seem to care, that it doesn't seem to affect them in the same way it affects me? When those things that fall under the remit of the mental load aren't done, why am I the only one who feels anxious, discombobulated and unsettled while the rest of my family just get on with their day?

I don't know, but I do know that if I'm the only one experiencing something, then at least part of it is a *me* problem. Sure, the people I love and live with need to step up and take care of their side of the street more, but also, maybe I need to step off their side of the street more and focus on my own? It's possible that, within the microcosm of my own house, I need to step back and – here's the rub – learn to *be okay with the idea that a little litter here and there isn't the end of the world*. I can, I realise, *choose* to be okay with the dishes piling up occasionally or the floor being a bit dirty. I can perhaps choose to accept imperfections on a very real and tangible level rather than see them as signs that I am, somehow, failing. I can meet my family halfway and maybe, in doing so, it'll give them the space to rise up and meet me in the middle too.

Of course, there were times when I wasn't wrong, or to blame, and good lord did I indulge in the glory of that, but it wasn't a win, even though I tried to sell it to myself like that. It wasn't a win because, contrary to the way I behaved, we hadn't signed up for a lifelong marital version of *Squid Games*, where we lived in a constant state of fight or flight. We had, in fact, signed up for a life together. At some point, while we dated, we had assessed each other on a million different levels and decided that doing life together would be better, easier, more fun, than it would be to do it alone. I don't know when that decision to be a team turned into a decision to 'Hunger Games' the shit out of it all and see who came out alive, but somehow, somewhere, that's what happened.

10

The Sock that Broke
the Camel's Back

'How often it is that the angry man rages denial of
what his inner self is telling him.' – *The Woman in White*,
Wilkie Collins

At the time I told Jimmy that we were separating, if you'd have
asked me, I would have told you *he* was the problem in our
marriage without hesitation. If you'd hooked me up to a lie
detector and asked me the same question, I'd have passed the
test with flying colours, because I truly believed that I was
right. There wasn't one thing I could point to and say, 'Look
at what he did! Of course I want a separation.' Instead, it was
a slow, subtle and insidious montage of things. It was divorce
by a thousand paper cuts except the cuts were socks left lying
around or constant questions about where things were.

Why can't he just get with the programme? I used to lament
to myself, in my head, where no one else could hear it. *Why
can't he just see what needs to be done?* I used to whisper under
my breath, behind a locked bathroom door while I fought
back tears and wished, wished, he just *knew* what my mental
load entailed. Was I the only one who saw the mess, the dirt,

the dust? Was I the only one who cared about changing the bed, or was capable of changing the bed? Was it really so hard to put a load of laundry on without shrinking something? Was helping me keep track of all appointments and clubs and birthdays too much to ask? I truly believed that he wasn't as 'evolved' as I was, or that men weren't as evolved as women were. I believed he didn't get it, or if he did, he was wilfully ignoring it because he didn't want to do it.

Looking back, I can be brutally honest with myself about my part in the whole thing, and it always, *always* comes back to communication. There was a gaping chasm between what I thought he knew or, more accurately, what I *wanted* him to know and what he actually knew about how I was feeling. The thought of having a conversation with him about it, before it erupted into a crisis, felt like a loss to me somehow, and my pride wasn't ready to stoop that low. I'd somehow equated his ability to read my mind and to know what I needed and wanted as evidence that he loved me. Having to tell him what to do felt like having to tell him how to love me – and shouldn't he just know?

The reality is, I don't think I wanted him to succeed. I think I just wanted him to understand how hard it was. It wasn't really about looking for a solution. Instead, if I'm honest, it was about getting him to see how hard I worked, to feel sorry for me, perhaps even to feel a little indebted to me. I felt taken for granted and in response I wanted him to *feel* the pain and frustration I was feeling. Talking to him about it was the grown-up, solution-seeking thing to do, but my resentments were so acute that I just wanted to cause the same kind of chaos for him that I'd been experiencing.

Amid this domestic battle (that he didn't even really know we were engaged in), I was so desperate for him to be a worthy opponent that I didn't even consider what it would be like if we were on the same team. My instinct isn't to be part of a team. I think a lot of this comes from being an only child and going to boarding school at eleven. I was never a pack animal. I felt alone a lot as a child, so I got used to walking through the world solo. At boarding school, I struggled with severe homesickness. For the first six months, I cried from the moment I woke up until the minute I went to sleep, including through every lesson. At first, my school mates were sympathetic, but after a while, they understandably got bored of my relentless misery. I would call my parents four or five times a day, begging them to let me come home. *You'll be okay*, they'd say. *It'll pass. You'll learn to love it,* my mum once said to me. The only thing I learned was that when I cried and asked for help, no one came. After a term and a half, I returned to school after February half term and the crying had just stopped. I remember telling my therapist that I was okay after that.

'I'm not sure you were okay,' she said hesitantly. 'I think you were like those Romanian orphans. You just stopped crying because you realised no one was going to come.' To this day, that assessment of what really happened still makes me emotional.

I had tried asking for help once and I wasn't about to make that mistake again. So, rather than take the chance that Jimmy would hear me and want to help me when I told him I was in pain, or I was afraid, I would come out guns blazing. On the flip side, Jimmy did not thrive in that kind of constant conflict. Rather than lean into combat, he'd start to bend himself to be and do what he thought I wanted. If I wasn't happy, he wouldn't allow himself to be happy. I detested that side of him. I saw it as neediness, and as someone who'd grown up believing fiercely that the only person you could rely on was yourself, his willingness to hand me his power was sickening. This also wasn't a healthy response, and it took us years to realise that both of us were responding to the same trauma of abandonment in very different ways.

My frustration could be boiled down to one simple question: *Why can't he just be as good as me at recognising the mental load and acting accordingly?*

Well, there were three reasons. Firstly, I'd made the mistake of assuming telepathy was a reliable form of communication. Secondly, I positioned us as opponents, rather than teammates. And thirdly? Well, I was expecting him to be good at something he'd never been trained to do. Whether I liked that fact or not, I had to learn not to let myself be distracted or angered by the existential failings of society and deal with the issue that lay in the microcosm of my own house, my own family. If I wanted Jimmy to be an effective teammate, I was going to have to give him the space and grace to learn and not kneecap him with shame before he'd even given it a shot.

Of course, all of those insights only became clear to me with the gift of hindsight. It didn't occur to me to have a conversation with him about it. Instead, I felt like his inability to 'just know' was an indication of the fact that he didn't love me, or that we were, in some way, completely incompatible. If it had occurred to me, I wouldn't have had the wherewithal to address it in a calm and quiet moment. Why? I'm not an idiot – I know that would have been the best time to do it – but when things were calm, it's because, somehow, I was coping. And when I was managing, the conversation didn't feel like one that had to happen, so instead, I'd wait until I was all out of patience and fucks and *then* I'd lose my shit and decide that the time for a come-to-Jesus chat was now.

The confusing thing for Jimmy and the kids was that the cause of my shit-loss wouldn't be some atrocious, domestic crime. No. It would be because I'd come across that one sock thrown in the general direction of the laundry bin but not quite in, or one pair of shoes carelessly flung on the floor. I wouldn't see a sock or a pair of shoes, though. I'd see a big fucking neon sign that said, 'I don't have to do this mundane task because that stupid bitch will do it' alongside a flashing arrow pointing to me. And with that, my body would get hot instantly, the rage would rise, the beast would awaken and seven shades of hell would be unleashed upon my husband, who would stand there, *baffled* by my overreaction to what he saw, which was, of course, just a single sock on the floor.

Of course, every time I exploded with rage over a single sock, it was about more than that one sock. That sock was a representation of all the socks and shoes and underpants that had gone before. It was the spark that lit the fuse of the resentment bomb that I'd been building piece by piece for weeks, or at least since my last explosion. That sock was just the confirmation I needed to prove what I had suspected: that Jimmy didn't care about me, he didn't keep me in mind, he didn't respect me and he probably didn't even like me, but he kept me around to pick up his fucking socks. That sock was the sock that broke the camel's back, but my husband didn't know that because rather than talk to him about the fact that I was feeling overwhelmed and disrespected and not kept in mind, I collected those resentments like spiky trinkets, swallowing them down until I vomited them all out, all at once.

It took me years to recognise the pattern:

ME	HIM
I'm okay, I've got this.	*Looks around* Everything seems fine.
↓	↓
I'm tired and I need some help.	She looks a bit tired. I hope she's okay.
↓	↓
Why can't he see I need some help?	She'd ask if she needed help.
↓	↓
Why isn't he fucking helping?	Last time I helped, I did it all wrong so …
↓	↓
He's a dick and I don't know why I married him.	Wow. She's being a real bitch.
↓	↓
I'm regretting all my life decisions.	I'm regretting all my life decisions.
↓	↓
Everything is too much. It's too hard. I can't do it.	Everyone take cover. She's going to blow.
↓	↓
Door slamming, screaming, shouting, crying,	Door slamming, screaming, shouting, crying,

THE SOCK THAT BROKE THE CAMEL'S BACK

'I can't do this anymore'
on repeat.

↓

Massive fight that's been
brewing for ages.

↓

Exhausted talk about my
feelings and his feelings.

↓

Apologies.

↓

Things are better for a bit.

↓

I'm okay, I've got this.

Rinse and repeat.

'I can't do this anymore'
on repeat.

↓

Massive fight that came out of
nowhere.

↓

Finally an explanation for
what's been going on.

↓

Apologise. Promise to do
better.

↓

I'm doing better.

↓

Looks around Everything
seems fine.

It was only when we were in counselling that our therapist gently suggested that perhaps we could save ourselves a lot of hard work, emotional trauma and aggressive exchanges if it went more like this:

I'm okay, I've got this.

↓

I'm tired and I need some help.

↓

Looks around Everything
seems fine.

↓

She looks a bit tired. I hope
she's okay.

↓

Ask for some help and be clear about what you need.

Listen to what she needs and do it with joy in my heart and a smile on my face.

↓ ↓

Ah, that's better. I feel supported.

This is actually quite a lot. I need to remember that I'm 50% responsible for this shit.

↓ ↓

He's a great guy. I'm glad I married him.

I'm lucky to have her. We rock.

End scene.

And so, my lack of communication, my pride, my predilection for martyrdom, my desire to control, was my part in it. But what was his part in it?

Well, when the women in men's lives go apoplectic because they've come across their own version of the single sock lying on the floor, close to the laundry bin, but not quite in it, the men say, 'Well, you should have asked for help,' or the slightly less aggressive, 'Why didn't you ask for help?' And they're not wrong, but they're also not without responsibility in this relational fracture. Because of their lack of domestic conditioning, men generally, and genuinely, often don't know *how* to help, but they'd rather scoop their own kidney out and pour chilli pepper in the gaping hole than admit that they don't know how to do something as menial as fold towels properly, or make a bed, or clean the kitchen. And that's part of the problem: the tasks that come under 'the mental load' have been minimised and reduced to 'women's work'. Suggesting that your male partner might not know how to do tasks he sees as beneath him and his place in this society, even on a subconscious level, can lead to pretty fraught interactions.

I've tried and tested many different ways to walk on the eggshells surrounding Jimmy, in my efforts to suggest that he could do the laundry in the way that I've taken years to establish as the most efficient way, and none of them have really worked, if I'm honest. He'll freely admit that he's not good at being teachable at the best of times, but there's something more emotionally flammable when it's your wife that's the teacher. It's like when a parent tries to teach their teenager to drive – it always ends in tears. That parent might even be a fully qualified driving instructor, but it won't matter. We don't like being taught by the people we are closest to. Accepting you don't know how to do something is a vulnerability that a lot of us, for whatever reason, don't feel comfortable exposing to our nearest and dearest.

The final and perhaps the most important thing I've learned from spending many years in conflict with my husband over the management of the mental load in all its forms is this: I had to remind myself to focus on my part in it. I would self-indulgently recount to myself and anyone else who would listen the long, long list of things my husband did that were wrong or selfish or thoughtless. My diatribe about Jimmy would roll off the tongue, fluently. It would act as a kind of salve on the very real pain and anxiety I felt about the fact that my relationship was disintegrating, one discarded sock at a time. And, while it was easier to focus on his failings, I never considered that I had any failings of my own.

Admitting that I played a part in it felt unfair. Even if I

could admit it was true, my part wasn't as big or as bad as his part in it. But I figured out – way too late – that it wasn't about who did what wrong. It was about recognising that I couldn't make him do things differently, but I could make *myself* do things differently. And, if I recognised that my part in it was not communicating properly, I could change that and try a different approach. After all, the approach I'd been taking wasn't exactly working . . . so why not try something new? And maybe, just maybe, if I tried something new, then it would elicit a new response from Jimmy?

I didn't know for sure that it would work, but I had to take a leap of faith and trust that the man I'd married wasn't the irredeemable dickhead I'd come to believe he must be. I needed to trust that if I behaved differently, he might too, because the silent truth was, I didn't like who I'd become. I didn't like who I was when I was vomiting the rage, or silently seething. I didn't like the thoughts that went through my head, or the things I'd say out loud to friends and family. It wasn't a version of myself that I liked or wanted to be known for and so, even if it was for that reason alone, I wanted to try an approach to the situation that made me feel proud of myself and that didn't make me feel like I'd let myself down.

11

Addicted To . . . Everything

'Women have come a long way over the past twenty years, but in substance abuse and addiction, women have come the wrong way.' – Joseph A. Califano Jr

Here's a fact that won't shock you: scientists only started researching the effects of substance abuse on women in the 90s. Up until that point – despite centuries of evidence to suggest that addiction didn't just affect men – any and all research had only been carried out on the male of the species. It's hard to know whether they simply made the assumption that men's and women's bodies were more or less the same and therefore would react in the same way, or whether they just didn't give much of a shit. Actually, scratch that – it's not hard to know; it's terrifyingly easy.

If you ask me – and you're reading this book, so I'm going to assume that, implicitly, you did – one of the main reasons addiction in women between the ages of thirty and fifty is on the rise has to be connected to the mental load and the exponential growth of responsibility that women have taken on. There are clear links between anxiety and depression and substance abuse and I suspect (in a very non-scientific way) that the reported figures of women abusing alcohol don't even touch the sides of the *real* numbers of women abusing alcohol.

Women are great at masking. We mask when we're upset, we mask when we're feeling threatened or uncomfortable, we mask our anxiety, we mask our insecurities, we mask our hormone imbalances, our neurodivergences. We are experts at creating coping mechanisms to ensure that we don't expose our vulnerabilities, whether they be physical, physiological or emotional. Why? Because we want to survive this world that is, categorically, not designed with us in mind. Historically, women who kicked up a fuss got burned at the stake, so those of us with an X chromosome learned, pretty damn quickly, that fitting in was key.

Fitting in, by the way, doesn't mean being accepted as an equal. Women still, to this day, don't enjoy that level of acceptability. Instead, 'fitting in' has and continues to mean nothing more than not being a pain in the ass when it comes to the way men want the world to work. I truly believe that part of women's inability to relinquish the mental load is a fear, on a genetically subconscious level, that it will render women less useful to the point of being obsolete in a patriarchal society. If value in this world is 'usefulness' on a practical level, which is what our society is built on, with little regard for the emotional, cerebral and mental elements of caring and surviving, then what use are women if we're not cooking dinner? And so, we continue to fight back and claim some space for ourselves, while being unable to detach ourselves from the historically induced fear that if we let our responsibilities at 'home' go, we will eventually die out.

The problem with fitting in, with being a woman born in the twenty-first century, but also inheriting generational survival strategies, is that it's exhausting. It means that we are physically running around all over the place, splitting ourselves into many, many parts so that we can be wherever we need to be, whenever we need to be there. But it also means that we're constantly digging deep to be polite and patient and kind and funny and have a clean house and look good and make sure we don't, heaven forbid, age at a natural and, hence, unacceptable rate.

The mental load is an inevitable consequence of making ourselves acceptable in a world that requires us to prove our usefulness in a practical sense and deal with the pressures that come with that, as well as the lack of space to speak up about it. If they are able to say it out loud, and maybe even ask for help, the limited support available to women in managing the monumental weight of the responsibility and expectation that has been placed upon them cannot, in my opinion, be underestimated when it comes to discussions about the rise in addiction among women.

According to studies done at Harvard, girls between the ages of twelve and seventeen are more likely to misuse all types of prescription opioids and stimulants than boys of the same age.[3] Without even looking at the context around this, as a woman I am willing to bet that social pressure to behave a certain way, social media, being in unsafe situations and feeling a lack of care and support are bound to play a huge part in this.

On a personal level, my lack of self-worth played a huge part in the disintegration of my relationship and my subsequent slide into alcoholism. At the very base of it all was the firm belief that I wasn't worth anyone's real time, or real love, or real care, or real sacrifice. I felt uncomfortable asking for help because, when people did help, it somehow felt like I was tricking them, hoodwinking them into thinking I was worthy of their help, like they didn't really know what a piece of shit I really was.

This absence of my own self-worth isn't down to a specific trauma or any particular experience. I don't think it was eliminated by someone or something because, in actual fact, I don't believe it was ever there. I think a lot of women – maybe all of us to a greater or lesser extent – struggle to feel worthy of taking up space, not just in this world but also in the heads and hearts of the people we share this world with. We are generationally trained to make ourselves small, insignificant and not a pain in the ass. It's a survival thing. It's why, I believe, on some subconscious level, we readily take on the shackles of the mental load, because on an evolutionary level, it means women are useful, indispensable in a world that has done all it can to ensure we never step into our full power, that we never understand our true worth in the grand scheme of things.

We've all heard about the perils of 'wine o'clock'. I bought into it in a big way when I became a parent. If you've followed me on social media for a while, you'll know that the shift to parenting was not an easy one for me and that didn't exactly do wonders for my self-worth. I felt like I was incapable of doing what I'd been told was my ultimate destiny. The fetishisation of motherhood was something I fell foul of and while we can talk about unrealistic beauty standards and body standards, not enough people are talking about unrealistic standards of motherhood. A drink at the end of yet another day of being a shit mum was the numbing nectar I craved.

It's easy to see where my drinking turned into alcoholism. The first year of being a mum was the hardest thing I've ever done. I was alone a lot, my family lived 200 miles away, I didn't have any friends locally apart from the ones I made at playgroup and I can't classify those women as real friends because, honestly, I wasn't my real self. I had no idea how I'd ended up spending my mornings in dusty church halls, grasping a shit cup of coffee and a soggy custard cream talking about sleep training and pretending to give a shit. It wasn't that I didn't give a shit about my baby, but I really struggled to connect with other women when all they talked about was babies.

If you're trying to be the perfect mother, you lose part of yourself. You lose the real part of yourself. You lose the part that knows it's okay to do things how you want to do them, the part that you can trust instinctively. You question everything you were and everything you thought – and what's left over is a sleep-deprived, lost, little-girl soul wondering how you can ever recover. That's how I felt anyway. I felt like everything I'd done up to that point had been a waste of time, because when I finally did something that really mattered – have a baby – I was shit at it. Those feelings, constantly, start to take their toll, and wine helped.

I would play with baby toys, read baby books, change baby nappies, cook baby food, pack baby bags, clean up baby mess and maybe women better than me were able to find the joy and gratitude in that, but I couldn't. That's on me – I've learned that self-pity is the slippery slope, and while things were hard and I wasn't fully supported, I leaned into that self-pity, rather than admit I was struggling and ask for help.

I drank a lot of wine. After I'd put my daughter to bed, and before I tackled the mess in the house that the day had left behind, I'd open a bottle of Malbec. I'd drink the first glass while scrolling through social media and then I'd put my headphones in, find some mind-numbing programme to watch on my phone and move around the house clearing up the day's detritus. I'd return, intermittently, to the kitchen to refill my glass. A bottle of wine was easy to finish. I'd often start a second bottle but, on a normal night, I'd never quite finish it. Not because I didn't want to, but because I knew I wasn't an alcoholic if I left a bottle of wine unfinished.

The reality was, I was lonely and scared, I didn't feel seen or heard and I had severe postnatal depression, but what those things felt like was anger. I was angry all the time. I was angry at Jimmy for always being away, I was angry at myself for being so fucking useless as a human, a woman and a mother. I was angry at my family for living so far away and not offering to help more. I was angry that we weren't rich and that we couldn't afford a nanny or to do our shopping at Waitrose (which was the closest supermarket). But the truth was, I wasn't capable of understanding what I was really feeling. It looked a lot like I was angry, but that was just a show. My anger – in fact *all* my bad behaviour – was a mask, a shield that I flung around the house in an effort to distract everyone from what I was really feeling, which was almost certainly fear or pain.

At that time, the wine felt like a girlfriend who didn't mind hearing me bitch and moan, relentlessly, about how hard my life was and who co-signed everything.

Here's the thing about alcoholism – it doesn't always look the way you think. It's not always old men on benches, with string holding up their trousers and a bulbous, red nose. It's not always angry men or violent men or dangerous men. It's not always sloppy women who can't get out of their dressing-gowns and neck a bottle of vodka they hid in the laundry cupboard before breakfast. It *can* be those things, but that wasn't what it was for me and it's not what it was for many of the other women in recovery that I know and love.

For me, alcoholism was slow and insidious. It was cunning and baffling. I never drank in the mornings, I was never drunk at work, I didn't get arrested, I didn't lose my licence, I didn't lose my marriage or my kids. People didn't look at me with pity and whisper behind my back about how they wished I would get help. Most people were shocked when I went into recovery. A lot of people told me I wasn't an alcoholic. Some thought I was just being dramatic. But I was drinking at least a bottle of wine most nights. The nights I didn't drink – maybe one or two nights a week – were proof, in my mind, that I didn't have an alcohol problem. Those dry nights were the answer to the question, on repeat, in my head, that I kept trying to ignore: *Do you think you've got an alcohol problem?* And I'd tell myself no, I didn't have an alcohol problem, because an alcoholic wouldn't be able to go a night without booze, right?

Wrong.

When I drank that first drink, whether it was in the evening, or when I went out, or when I was in an airport or whenever, the truth is, I had no idea when I would stop. Mostly, if I was at home, I would stop at just shy of two bottles. I'd be drunk but not paralytic and I wouldn't have blacked out. It would be more than enough to make me feel shit the next morning. But, if I was out, there was no stopping me. In the history of my drinking, I never, ever went out, had a glass of wine or two and came home. Or, if I did, I'd have another glass when I got home.

I didn't drink every day, but I thought about drinking all the time. If I didn't have a glass of wine in my hand, I knew when I was going to get one and, if I didn't know when I was going to get one, I'd make plans stat, to ensure that a legitimate reason for drinking was just around the corner. I surrounded myself with people who liked to drink and use drugs in the same way I did. I said inane things like, *I don't trust people who don't drink*. I wasn't an angry drunk or a violent drunk. Sure, when I got home I'd start an argument with Jimmy, but as far as everyone else knew, I was nothing more than a party girl who knew how to have a good time.

Behind closed doors, both literally and metaphorically, I was of course fucking miserable. No one knew; I didn't even know really. I just thought this was how life was now and so I drank heavily in the evenings because it felt like I deserved it, because it made me feel better and because I fucking loved it. At no point did I truly believe it was a problem, even though, if I'm honest, there was always a little voice inside me that questioned everything.

Really, though, it wasn't the daily drinking that was the problem. The problem was the binge drinking. It was the nights off or the nights out that caused the problems. These were the nights when I could let loose because I'd been set free. Maybe I had a babysitter, or a grandparent had come to watch the girls, or maybe it was because Jimmy was home. Whatever the situation, one thing was true – I felt free from the shackles of being a solo parent or a parent at all. The responsibility of looking after small children, while working, while running a household and all that entailed, was temporarily gone. And I mean gone. I never approached a night out like a temporary reprieve from which I would return refreshed and ready to get on with the graft. I didn't consider any consequences; I just went all out. It felt like I had a short window of opportunity to enjoy myself and I would press the fuck-it button.

Sometimes, I'd get out without any significant consequences. More often than not, I'd lie to my husband because I'd tell him I'd be home at midnight and not get home until 6am. Or, he'd call me to find out where I was and I'd ignore the call or just say that I was on my way home but that the tubes were all fucked up. I'd frequently lose my debit card, or my phone, or my bag, and it would be a drama getting home. I'd occasionally fall asleep in taxi cabs and I'm just eternally grateful that none of those drivers ever did anything awful to me.

Occasionally bad things would happen. I'd have to fight off men I'd been shamelessly flirting with because I thought it was all good, drunken fun. One followed me all the way back to my tube station. I was once sexually assaulted by a man I worked with. I came to from a blackout in his hotel room and his fingers were inside me. It was the single most terrifying thing that happened to me. I pushed him off, grabbed my stuff and ran for my life. I was found sobbing in the foetal position in the lift. The police were called. A rape kit was done. I didn't press charges.

There are things I did while I was drinking that I am far from proud of. I'd get other people to pick up my kids because a 'work meeting' was running late, when in reality, I'd been having a boozy lunch and wanted to chase the buzz for as long as possible. I was a binge drinker – once I started I didn't know when I was going to stop, where I was going to end up or if I was going to be okay. But I kept doing it. I think half of the problem was that I equated getting absolutely shitfaced with 'me time' and (hilariously) self-care. I felt enti- tled to it, and because that time was so scarce, when it came, I was going to give it my all. The other half of the problem was that I am an addict – through and through. I may not have looked like one from the outside, but take away booze and, unless I'm really vigilant, I'll get addicted to anything else if it changes the way I feel. Except running. For some reason, I haven't become addicted to running yet. Annoyingly.

The fact is, my self-worth was so low and I was so unhappy that I was desperate to change the way I felt all the time and in any way. It wasn't the mental load's fault; it was because I was so incapable of understanding what I was really feeling at any given time and even less capable of communicating that to anyone that I just used booze and drugs as a way of avoiding it altogether. As Taylor Swift says, *I'm the problem, it's me.*

When the consequences of my drinking only affected me, it was easy to lock them away in a box labelled 'DENIAL'. But, when the consequences of my drinking began to affect other people – people I professed to love – I was forced to question whether my drinking was, in fact, 'normal'. In recovery, I finally understand that grown-up life, with all its responsibilities and sacrifices is tough, and you can either put your big girl pants on and get vulnerable and learn to communicate and accept criticism and do better next time, or you can get shitfaced every weekend and blow up your life.

Sharing my story is hard and painful and I'm sure many of you will be shocked and disgusted by my admissions, and you're right to be. But I have no doubt that others reading this will find themselves breathing a sigh of relief, alongside the shock and disgust, because they too have shameful secrets that they've been too afraid to speak of. It is in that recognition, that relatability, that we let go of judgement and find compassion.

I'm also aware of how my privilege plays into my ability to make this confession. Let's not beat around the politically correct bush here. The fact that I'm white, middle class and ticking a lot of socially acceptable boxes just by the very nature of where, when and to whom I was born means that, rightly or wrongly, I receive more leniency when it comes to this sort of thing. I'm not saying it's ever considered acceptable, but if I was a woman of colour, a single mum and living in a council house, disclosures like the ones I've just made would be received by a lot of people in a very different way. Some of the things I did while drinking were wrong, no matter who I am, but I have a responsibility as someone who is given more grace in general, to use that grace to be honest about addiction and where it takes you. The one thing we can give addiction credit for is its commitment to inclusivity. No one is immune.

I don't know why I ended up with the disease of addiction

and, honestly, it doesn't really matter. There's enough evidence to suggest that this is a hereditary affliction, so I'm sure genetics loaded the gun, but there's no doubt in my mind that the trauma of my first birth and my subsequent declining mental health played a significant part in pulling the trigger. Add to that my inability to cope with the 'do it all/have it all' expectations I felt, the weight of the mental load and my belief that I was only worth something if I was the best at something (or, if I'm honest, everything), and it's no surprise that I clung to the one thing that allowed me to escape that pressure, even if only temporarily.

It's down to pure luck that the consequences of my drinking weren't more serious. I'm no less of an alcoholic because of that. I was just fucking lucky. I lived my life on a knife edge and it was through no doing of my own that I somehow kept coming down on the right side of it. I am thankful every day that I got out of the cycle of dangerous drinking before the consequences became irreparable and, trust me, they would eventually have become irreparable. Once you start craving the effects of alcohol – the cold, crisp first sip of a Sauvignon Blanc or the warm, comforting salve of a Malbec – it doesn't go away. It'll always get stronger – sometimes quickly, sometimes slowly – but always and eventually, it'll take you over.

If you're reading this and worried about your own alcohol use, then all I can tell you is that when it comes to my mental health, my ability to manage the mental load, to be present, to communicate with my husband in a constructive way and to be at the top of my game, giving up alcohol was the best thing I've ever done. This isn't about preaching to you, but it is my experience that alcohol never added anything to my life, not really. Sure, it wasn't all bad, but it wasn't as good as it could have been . . . as it is now.

People think I'm insane when I say this, but I'm so grateful that I am an alcoholic and even more grateful that I found recovery. Sure, active addiction was horrendous – the kind of pain I wouldn't wish on anyone – but recovery has opened my world up in a way I could never have expected and in a way it never would have done if my life hadn't hung in the balance. I would never have found the humility I have now if it wasn't for recovery. I wouldn't have found the 'village' I have now if it wasn't for recovery. My marriage wouldn't be as strong as it is now without recovery and my ability to write this book (and hopefully others!) wouldn't be possible without recovery. My ability to manage the world I move through – including all the pressures of being a wife, a mother, a business owner, a sister, a friend and everything else – would be chaotic if it wasn't for sobriety.

Building a solid sobriety has meant that I have been able to slowly extricate myself from what had become a co-dependent relationship in a lot of ways. I was relying on Jimmy to make me happy and when he didn't do the things I thought he should do, I was pissed off at him. It never occurred to me that I was responsible for my own happiness and, in turn, Jimmy was responsible for his. I still struggle with this. When I sense that Jimmy is feeling down or struggling, I get an anxious feeling in my tummy. It's hard for me to let go and get on with my day. I have an overwhelming urge to fix it by making him laugh, or making him lunch, and when that doesn't fix his mood, I get annoyed. My sobriety has taught me that I can be confident that his bad mood is not about me, and if it is, it's his responsibility to let me know, not mine to eke it out of him. It has also meant that I can confidently get on with my day and wait for him to ask for help or just give him the space to sort himself out. No need to make it about me at all.

Sobriety isn't a process with a beginning and an end. It's a daily battle that starts from scratch every time I open my eyes in the morning. It starts with taking a minute, before I even get out of bed, to check in with myself. I mentally scan my body and try to be clear about how every inch of it feels. Do I feel tired? If I do, then I know I have to be gentle with myself and vigilant of the vulnerability that tiredness exposes. Tiredness and lack of rest are, for me, kryptonite to my sobriety and my ability to manage my actions and reactions. I try to pinpoint any thoughts that are causing me anxiety and be honest about whether I'm dealing with them appropriately or not. I am exceptionally skilled in burying my head in the sand, isolating myself, turning inwards when things are worrying me. I'd always rather deal with them myself, ride out the storm in secret and only talk about it when it's over.

Maintaining my sobriety in a world that loves nothing more than to bury women in unrealistic expectations has been, I believe, the keystone of finding a sense of peace that has allowed me to exist in a partnership without constantly feeling the need to blow it all up. The mental load is an easy-to-reach grenade for us as women, as is a bottle or two of Malbec, and we reach for it, not because we want him to do more laundry, but because we want to know that they care about us, they care that we are upset, or struggling. We want to know that, without being asked or nudged, they are keeping us in mind.

I think my point is this: sometimes it's helpful to think of the mental load, and the feelings it elicits within your relationship, as a symptom of bigger problems. I know that doesn't sound very positive, but in some ways, I truly believe it is. If, as women, we continue to think that all the issues in our marriages and relationships would simply be solved if he would just remember to put the loo seat down, or bother to learn the names of our children's paediatricians, I think we'd find that those things didn't fix anything. I truly believe that, as a generation, we've never been taught to be comfortable with truly trusting someone, opening up to them, giving ourselves to them and having faith that they value us enough to do the right thing, even if it's boring or hard. We have been led to believe that strong foundations are great sex, or magical moments that we post on Instagram, when actually, the strongest foundation of all is learning how to keep someone in mind and trust that they will do the same thing for you. And, more than that, that every single morning, you'll both wake up and choose to keep doing that, over and over again until the 'death do us part' phase of this whole thing kicks in.

While my sobriety is solid, I'd be lying if I said my self-worth always is. I still have a very wobbly sense of self-worth on a general level, but within my marriage I have grown to believe that I do matter enough to ask Jimmy to meet me halfway, to take the time and energy to hold my heart and mind with care. That's important, because it gives me the courage to have difficult conversations with him about things like not feeling supported in the day-to-day running of our lives and to trust that he will want to dig deep to do the hard thing and listen with good intentions because I'm important enough to him. I've learned to trust that he actually *does* want to be with me and therefore wants to do the work to make that happen.

I've learned to trust that my feelings do matter and that they are valid but I've had to figure out what those feelings really are, and removing alcohol was a huge step in revealing them. It's also allowed me to take time to express my feelings in a way that isn't totally c*nty. I know now that my anger was never my husband's problem to manage or fix.

When it comes down to it, my life is better, easier, calmer and less painful without alcohol in it. It's that simple.

12

Burn, Baby Burn

'Relaxing brings weakness when done by a muscle; but brings strength, when done by a person.' – Mokokoma Mokhonoana

Mum burnout (or Depleted Mother Syndrome) is something I've only heard formalised as an actual thing in recent months, but it's something I've struggled with since my babies splashed down earthside. Mum burnout is a recognised state of emotional, physical and mental depletion when the mental and physical load of being a mother, a wife, an employee, a taxi service, a nurse and therapist gets too much. It's the painful culmination of running on empty, of giving everything and getting little in return, of cooking food that is sneered at, of running everywhere and still being late, of sacrificing an hour of sleep for an hour of peace, of negotiating arguments, managing everyone's schedules, remembering to take the bins out and getting the big food shop done. It is the inevitable crash landing for women who bear the weight of the mental and physical load of 'adulting' with little or no support.

According to a study published in *Clinical Psychological Science,* parental burnout is characterised by three key symptoms: *emotional exhaustion, emotional distancing* and *parental inefficacy.* In layman's terms: feeling knackered, totally unable to give a shit, and spending so much time beating yourself up for it that you can't even parent anymore. At heart, I am a perfectionist. Actually, it would be more accurate for me to say, *at the most toxic and broken parts of me, I am a perfectionist.* I've never met a stick I don't love to beat myself with, so the idea of admitting I'm exhausted, distant and useless is one that sits very unhappily with me. It's taken me a long time to understand that perfectionism isn't a characteristic that some of us are born with and others aren't. It's actually a trauma response.

For me, perfectionism grew from a belief that I was only loved, wanted and acceptable if my grades were perfect, if my medals were gold and not silver (remember, darling, second place is first loser), and if I was the prettiest girl in the room. In that sense, my desire for perfection was born from a deep-rooted and overwhelmingly powerful fear of rejection and abandonment. This perfectionism was applauded and praised on so many occasions that it became not just a way of life, but a way to *survive* life. And it worked, until it didn't.

As a kid, the things I needed to be perfect at were pretty minimal. The list amounted to keeping my room clean and tidy, doing well in my school work, being captain of the netball team and standing on the podium at every swim meet. It was manageable. As a teen, the list of things to perfect grew a little – exams needed to be aced, my friendship group needed to be enviable, boyfriends needed to be good-looking,

I needed to be good-looking, and my ever-changing body needed to be kept in check.

The problem is, as you grow up, the list of things you are responsible for also grows up with you, and the ability to do all of them perfectly becomes impossible. By the time I was a mother, I was quite literally harming myself by trying to be the perfect mother, home-keeper, cook, wife, friend, daughter, sister, writer, business owner. I was also trying to maintain the perfect body by going to the gym and eating perfectly. Perfection also included being successful in my work and, as many of us do, I assumed that success at work meant earning lots of money. I also, obviously, had to have the perfect child, the perfect husband, the perfect life. None of this was because I felt like I was better than everyone else. It was because I felt I *had* to be better than everyone else because that was the only way I would remain wanted, acceptable, loved.

My heart breaks for the woman I was in those times of early motherhood. I was like a squirrel on cocaine, trapped in the glare of oncoming headlights not knowing whether to shit or go blind. So, I continued blindly cleaning up all the shit and hoping that no one could actually see what the inside of my head and heart looked like. I kept things bright and shiny on the outside to distract them from the very real darkness that was going on inside me.

Becoming a mother wasn't the first thing that led me to burnout. On reflection, and in discussion with my psychiatrist during my ADHD assessment, I came to realise that burnout had been common throughout most of my adult life.

When I was twenty-six, I spent Christmas at home with my mum and dad. Usually, Christmases meant a full house, merriment, morning drinking, and sprouts forgotten in the Aga. But this year, for some reason, it was just the three of us. For someone who lived with the constant existential fear of being abandoned or not wanted, I found the idea that everyone wanted to spend Christmas somewhere else hard to handle. It felt personal that they weren't there and even more personal that no one had thought to invite me anywhere. Add to this undiagnosed ADHD that I'd been masking for many years, a high-pressure job as an English teacher, an unhealthy relationship with alcohol, and the realisation that my only presents that year were six pairs of black socks from my mum and a steering wheel lock from my dad (because, apparently, we weren't spending very much this year) sent me into a spiral. Of course, it wasn't about the presents, but the presents were the final nail in the coffin on the camel's back.

I collapsed – literally. I physically fell to the floor, and lay in the foetal position. I could barely breathe. I was fossilised with exhaustion and fear and a million other itchy feelings that I couldn't identify. All I knew was that I could not keep going. My parents were understandably concerned and managed to get me an emergency GP appointment on Boxing Day. The GP asked me the ten questions that everyone with suspected depression gets asked and wrote me a prescription for Prozac, and that was it. I was depressed. It was only fifteen years later, when my psychiatrist suggested that this wasn't depression but burnout that everything fell into place in my head. Of course that's what it was. The idea that I was depressed had never sat 100 per cent comfortably with me. It wasn't because I was ashamed of it; it just didn't feel like it told the whole story. Burnout, though – that felt much more akin to what I was feeling in those times.

In the meantime, though, the Prozac helped and eight months later I came off it and was fine until two years later when it happened all over again. I spent the following fifteen years in this cycle of collapse, take meds, come off meds, be fine, collapse. I don't know, then, why I wasn't more vigilant of my mental health when I became a mother. If, because of my addiction to perfection, I was so prone to burning out *without* the responsibility of children, then surely I was a prime candidate for mum burnout? It's easy to say this and even easier to beat myself up about it with the benefit of hindsight, but the reality is that being a new mum is all-consuming, and 99.9 per cent of all your thoughts are about someone else. It's hard to find a hot minute to pee alone, let alone to breathe deeply and feel your feelings and check in with your own mental health.

With motherhood came an exponential increase in the weight of my mental load, and with that, my life became entirely unmanageable. I held on here and there, but most of the time I was crying somewhere, or shouting at someone, or drinking myself numb, or tossing and turning in bed, unable to sleep but deathly tired. Life felt like I was constantly treading water in a vat of treacle and as I slowly drowned, the glossy life ring of perfection was always just out of reach. But I kept going because that's what we do, right? *Of course I'm tired and struggling*, I would say to myself, *I've got a small baby and a husband who's away all the time. If I wasn't feeling like this, something would be wrong.* I did everything I could to normalise that unmanageability because if I, for one second, considered the possibility that I couldn't do everything perfectly, I wouldn't just be admitting I was a shit human who didn't deserve love and care; I'd have to admit that I was a shit mum – that I was unable to do the most natural thing in the world – and that was a far more terrifying proposition.

I grasped on to this idea of *perfection = love* until my knuckles shone white and my fingers were raw and bleeding. I didn't just have to manage the mental load, I had to manage the mental load *perfectly*. The baby's lunches for nursery didn't just have to be made, they had to be packed beautifully, with a little handwritten note. Clothes couldn't just be washed, they had to be washed and ironed and organised. The house didn't have to just be tidy and clean enough, it had to be 'hotel' clean and tidy. It had to smell perfect, the lighting had to be perfect, the décor impeccable. Beds were made with hospital corners, pillows perfectly plumped, windows smear-free, bathrooms glistening. *If I can just make sure everything outside me is perfect, then, and only then, will I feel like I'm good enough,* I'd have on in my subconscious on repeat.

It's only after a ton of work and therapy that I can see that I was my own worst enemy, but at the time, I was certain that it was my husband. You could have waterboarded me with truth serum and I would have bet both my ovaries that *he* was the problem. He didn't do enough, he didn't see the mess, he didn't use his initiative, he didn't care. I had brainwashed myself into thinking that perfection was the *only* standard anyone with an ounce of self-respect should aim for. I was cult-like in my commitment to this theory. It didn't matter how much Jimmy tried to suggest that I could prioritise some things and let some things go. The idea of letting anything go filled me with such visceral fear that it felt like rage. *I wouldn't have to let things go if you could just help me!* I would scream. Jimmy tried to help but, even with two people, perfection is unattainable. I was setting us both up to fail, over and over again, every day, and I didn't realise it.

It's probably worth saying that, as desperate and ugly as my description of this time seems, a lot of this unmanageability was hidden, because it was internal. There were definitely some blow-out rows between Jimmy and I but, for the most part, we did a cracking impression of being happily married and as far as anyone else was concerned, I was doing fine. Just like Ross in *Friends,* I was *fine. Fine. I was fine.* Inevitably, I got to a point where I absolutely wasn't fine. I totally lost my shit. I dropped my basket. I lost my marbles. The handle? I flew off it. I went back on anti-depressants; I didn't know anything about burnout and once I levelled out again, I went straight back to doing the same thing.

I can only imagine how hard it was to live with me. Living up to my own expectations was impossible enough, but expecting someone else to live up to them as well must have been incredibly difficult for Jimmy. My psychopathic need for perfectionism extended to my kids, too, and I feel guilty because there are hangovers from that that I have to deal with to this day. If they didn't write a letter to Granny perfectly, they'd have to start again. If they painted and it went outside the lines, they weren't trying hard enough. If their behaviour wasn't perfect, then I'd get shouty. There were times, and I'm not proud of this, when I would be overcome by a rage so instant and hot, a rage that would flood my entire body from head to toe and explode in a way that I scared my kids. I scared myself too, and the shame I would feel afterwards was crippling. Of course, it was all part of the same thing – a desire for perfection in every facet of my life, because that's what kept me safe, and when that didn't happen, the profound fear that I would be rejected or abandoned would come out sideways as rage.

Billie, my eldest, definitely bore the brunt of this. She was there for my lowest moments and, bless her, it was never her responsibility to make me feel better or safer, but I put that, unknowingly, on her. As she got older, I saw she developed a real fear of making mistakes. There were many times when she would refuse to try something in case she couldn't do it perfectly, or messed it up in some way. As I did more therapy, I began to see that I had instilled that in her, because she wasn't just afraid to make mistakes, she was afraid to make mistakes around *me*. It breaks my heart to even write that, and I knew I had to make some changes.

So many of our conversations since then have been about how mistakes are human, how failing isn't the opposite of succeeding, but that they are both part of the same process of learning. I talk openly about the mistakes I make and what I learn from them and, of course, I apologised to her. When she was about nine years old, I sat her down and explained that I owed her an apology. I told her how I'd struggled when she was little and that I'd tried to be perfect at everything. I told her that I'd expected her to be perfect too and that it had harmed us both. I explained how I'd made the mistake of thinking that being perfect would mean everyone loved me and never wanted to leave me but that I was wrong. I said that I was sorry I'd made her feel like she couldn't make mistakes and that if she did, that I wouldn't love her. I told her there was nothing she could do that would ever make me not love her – there was no mistake or failure that could even begin to be stronger than the love I felt for her. Every now and again, I reiterate that apology when I see her spiralling because she's worried she's going to get into trouble for a minor infraction, and I suspect I will keep reiterating it until the day I die. I'm just glad I managed to change the narrative when I did.

The mental load of women – whether you have children or not – is monumental enough without convincing yourself that you have to do it perfectly. It took me years to understand that it's okay to let things go, to loosen your grasp on life. After I'd spent twenty minutes whingeing to my therapist about how Jimmy doesn't make the bed properly, or put things in the dishwasher or just *know* that the floor needs vacuuming, she said, 'What will happen if those things aren't done?'

'Well,' I said, in a confused tone, because the answer seemed painfully obvious to me, 'the house will be a mess and I'll have to clean it.'

'But what if *you* don't clean it either, what will happen?'

I was irritated by this point and we could both hear it clearly in my voice. 'Well, I . . . I'll . . . ' I stuttered. 'Well, the house will be a mess.'

'Yes, but *what will happen*?'

The bitch was goading me now, but the truth was, I didn't know the answer. In fact, scratch that. The real truth was that I *did* know the answer, but didn't want to say it, or admit it.

'I guess, nothing will happen.'

'Yes,' she replied thoughtfully, 'I think I agree. I don't think anything terrible will happen, will it?'

At the time I felt like she didn't understand me, that she wasn't listening, that she was being facetious. But really, she was poking holes in my fantasy that told me bad things would happen if my life didn't look perfect. I didn't walk out of that session fixed, but it planted a seed that, over the next few years, would germinate into something resembling balance.

13

Apparently, Couples' Therapy Isn't a Competition

'It's natural that people argue. It's part of intimacy. But you have to have a good system of repair. You need to be able to go back, if you've lost it, which happens, and say, "I brought in my dirty tricks, I'm sorry," or, "You know what, I realised I didn't hear a single word you said because I was so upset. Can we talk about it again?"'
– Esther Perel

Out of all the things I'm asked in DMs on Instagram when I talk about the breakdown and subsequent repair of my relationship with my husband, the most common question is, 'How did you get your husband to go to couples' therapy?' It breaks my heart a little every time I read the same question over and over again, because I was lucky. When I sat down and blindsided my husband with the news that we were separating, he was the one that begged me to give couples' therapy another chance. I didn't want to. I felt as if I'd been there, done that, got the (very expensive) t-shirt.

What changed my mind was something that a good friend of mine said to me. I had just told her Jimmy and I were separating and, after telling me how sad the news made her, she said, 'Promise me one thing. Promise me you'll do *everything* you can to save it before giving up. If your marriage falls apart, that's okay, but you *need* to be able – no, scratch that, you'll desperately *want* to be able to look your kids in the eye and tell them you tried everything to save your marriage to their daddy.' Let me tell you, that hit me in the solar plexus, and when I hung up the phone, I immediately called Jimmy and said I would go back to couples' therapy.

Of course, I didn't think going back to couples' therapy would change anything. My mind was set on separation. I was already looking at paint colours for the flat I was going to rent. I was thinking about how fun it might be to start dating. I had been so miserable in my relationship for so long that saying, 'I think we should separate' out loud had felt like the metaphorical switching on of the lights announcing my new, single status. I looked at going back to couples' therapy as something I just had to endure, the last hurdle in this clusterfuck of a marriage, the final hoop that needed jumping through. *I've survived everything else,* I thought with more than a few overtones of victimhood, *I can get through this.*

We'd tried therapy once before, and while it had helped at the time, it hadn't stopped us from sliding back into old, toxic habits and patterns. Jimmy and I are very different people because we are products of very different environments, and I think we always just assumed those traits that had been imposed upon us in a monkey-see-monkey-do kind of way were set in stone. I don't think it ever occurred to us that we could, individually, *choose* to change those things, to become different people, to choose different actions and reactions, to dig deep and *decide* to go against our first thought and consider another option. The path of least resistance on a personal level was, of course, simply doing what we'd always done, but there was no doubt that was causing significant resistance when it came to our relationship.

There are a few sayings that I spent years using and believing that I've since come to learn were absolute, total bollocks. Phrases like, 'I'm just saying it how it is' and 'I am who I am . . . deal with it' and 'If you don't like the way I do things or say things then that's your problem'. The idea that my bad behaviour, or unkind delivery, or total inflexibility was *someone else's* problem is wild to me now. Of course, we have to remain true to ourselves, but if we're doing that with anything less than absolute kindness, then the only thing that's true is that you're being kind of a dick. It's not that your feelings about something or someone aren't valid, but there's every chance that the way you're expressing it is absolutely not valid.

I'll say that again, because this changed my life when I heard it for the first time: *Your feelings are valid, but the way you're expressing them isn't.* It's a phrase I use with my kids now on a daily basis. You know when they're screaming and crying and shouting and there's a touch of the psychopath about them because, oh, I don't know, you asked them to take their shoes off? That's when I kneel down and give them a hug and say, *Babe, I get it. You're frustrated and angry and those feelings are valid, but the way you're expressing them isn't.* Sure, that makes me sound like a fucking perfect mother, but trust me – I've tried the red-hot-rage approach many, many times as well. It's just that since realising I don't have to behave or react in the way my lizard brain wants me to, my life has become much calmer (and my kids are much happier!).

But, before I learned all this stuff about not *having* to behave the way I'd always behaved, the thought of going to therapy gave me the shits. I'd tell friends that it was a waste of time and that I was only doing it so I could tell my kids I did everything to try to save my marriage. The fact is, I was shit-scared. Somewhere, deep inside me, I knew that if I did therapy properly, I'd have to admit and accept that I'd played a part in all this, that I wasn't as perfect or as self-sacrificing as I thought I was. The vulnerability it would take to get to that point and then the painful process of identifying my bad behaviour and taking responsibility for changing it were feelings I had no intention of going anywhere near.

The first time we did therapy, I cheated. I didn't do it on purpose, but that thing inside me that repelled itself away from any kind of vulnerability as a form of misguided protection, including admitting that I was wrong, was so strong that I played everyone in that room. Or, I thought I did. Of course, our therapist, Frieda,* probably saw straight through me, but I approached that first stint in therapy as a war I had to win. Every session was a battle and nine times out of ten, I came out on top, or so I thought.

Jimmy, as I've mentioned before, is generally a better human than I am and so while I was ducking and diving and manipulating the shit out of those first therapy sessions, he was actually being honest and vulnerable. He was taking responsibility, and rather than rise up to meet him there, I would

* Name has been changed to protect the individual

nod smugly and look at our therapist as if to say, 'See? This is what I'm dealing with! He's admitting it . . . finally!' I wasn't prepared, or even able, to identify my part in it, and while I'm ashamed of the way I managed that situation, I also can look back on that person and feel compassion. I'm not an inherently awful human being, but I was a damaged, sad and lonely one. I was ill-equipped and underprepared to exist honestly and vulnerably in a partnership and so, in the fear of being hurt, caught, exposed, I battened down the emotional hatches and let Jimmy take the fall.

If I'm honest, I don't remember much about what happened in those first sessions – the ones we did before I decided to separate. I think I was so busy playing the game, being tactical, that I don't actually know what went on. I just remember being desperate to do all I could to ensure that the spotlight didn't shine on the deepest, darkest corners of my soul. I slipped in and out of the shadows, leaving Jimmy to strip down to an emotional nakedness while we all watched on.

Going back to therapy was deeply uncomfortable for me, as I'd known it would be. We went back to the same therapist, which I'd resisted, but Jimmy had insisted. Of course I'd resisted! I didn't want to go back to the person who already knew my modus operandi. I wanted a clean slate – a new mark that I could play the same tricks on. There was no way Frieda was going to fall for my nonsense again and, honestly, my armoury had run dry, but I couldn't think of a good enough reason to convince Jimmy that starting over with someone new was best. Frieda had the back story of our relationship and, if I was serious about wanting to do everything I could to save our marriage, why wouldn't I choose someone who already knew us? It was a valid point.

When we went back into that room, the tension was palpable, and it was all emanating from me. My defences were as high as they'd ever been. In that moment, I hated Frieda because I thought she was self-righteous and, worse, I thought she favoured Jimmy. Of course, the *real* reason I hated her was fear: fear she'd see through me, fear she'd expose me, fear she was going to call me out on my bullshit. Despite his previous admissions of bad behaviour, Frieda hadn't turned around to me and said something like, *I'm so sorry you've been going through this with this absolutely useless excuse for a human. It must have been so hard.* No. Instead, she had comforted Jimmy and told him how hard it must have been for him to admit that, or how he should be proud of himself for finally being honest. So, when I walked into that room, I genuinely felt like I was walking into battle.

As I write this, it occurs to me that that's how I've always felt when walking into any situation. My whole life, the baseline of my beliefs has been that people are against me. That somehow, someway, they are out to bring me down, and it had been no different in my marriage up until that point. I couldn't trust that anyone really cared for me or about me. I couldn't believe that I was worth enough to be cared about, let alone made sacrifices for. In my mind, I believed I was worthless and unless I fought to the death, everyone else might suddenly realise that too. This was how I went into therapy – defiant, defensive and delusional.

But there was something different this time around. I knew that if this didn't work then divorce was the only option. We weren't messing around with an amicable and possibly temporary separation now and a cosy little flat down the road. There was a clear sense that it was shit-or-get-off-the-pot time, and despite my previous eagerness to embrace time apart, I wasn't sure that divorce, in all its ugliness, expensive admin and finality, was really what I wanted. After all, Jimmy was still the person I wished it had worked out with in a perfect world. It's just that this wasn't a perfect world.

This time, before I knew it, I was taking therapy seriously. I listened when Jimmy spoke and not just for the parts where he admitted he was wrong. I heard the pressure he'd been feeling – his version of the mental load that I hadn't considered before. I heard him talk about things from his childhood that I'd never known or really taken time to understand. I began to join the dots between the things Jimmy had experienced and the way he reacted to certain things and situations. There were some sessions where I barely spoke because Jimmy needed space to tell his story and some sessions where I did all the talking. Often, we didn't even discuss what was happening in the present, our marriage wasn't the topic of conversation. Instead, we would talk about the things that happened a long time ago, the things that we were bringing *into* our marriage. In short, I began to realise that it wasn't all about me.

As the sessions went on I stopped focusing on point scoring. I began to see that Frieda didn't hate me; she just hadn't been able to work with the version of me I was presenting. She wasn't judging me, she was actually patiently waiting for me to stop judging her. Slowly but surely, I took tentative steps towards honesty and vulnerability. I didn't fully trust that doing so wouldn't destroy me, but I started to see Jimmy's shoulders drop a little, his brow unfurrow, and I wondered if I could feel a little bit of that too. I knew that it was either open up, take this shit seriously and potentially save my marriage with the man I still loved, or get divorced. And so I jumped in.

It wasn't easy. In fact, it was really painful and messy and I felt angry all the time. It turns out that, when you do therapy properly, it's really, really hard. Therapy is a process. It's a little like chemotherapy for your relationship, where it feels worse before it feels better. For the first six weeks, Jimmy and I could barely look at each other, let alone feel like we were making progress. Frieda asked us to trust the process. She suggested that we didn't talk about anything other than what was strictly and logistically necessary to get through each day and save any other conversations for therapy. Left to our own devices, we couldn't be trusted to handle things in a way that wouldn't cause more damage, and so, each week when we left therapy, we'd sit silently in the car on the drive home. When we walked in through the front door and the kids were there, we did a really good impression of being excellent parents. As soon as the kids weren't there or were asleep, we'd spring away from each other, desperate to avoid any kind of conflict.

It took me weeks to begin to understand that I'd never really let Jimmy in. I know I keep going on about it, but my fear of being honest and vulnerable wasn't just severe, it was chronic, and it was the basis of all my problems. Every single last one. I can sit here and write a long and creative list about *why* that was the case, but the fact is, it doesn't matter why. Figuring out why is just another way to burn energy looking for someone or something else to blame. I began to see that that energy would be far better spent trying to change. Looking forward to how I could do things differently, rather than always looking back angrily at the things other people had done or said, was the cure to my disease of terminal rightness.

The other thing that couples' therapy showed me was that it wasn't about showing us what a perfect relationship was; it was actually about showing us individually how imperfect we both were and giving us the tools to manage those imperfections in ourselves and, crucially, not in each other. The goal wasn't to eliminate the irritations, the frustrations, the fights, the resentments. The goal was actually to give us the tools to repair those things quickly and responsibly so that they didn't poison the air between us. For those of you who are way more evolved and self-aware than I ever was, then this may sound obvious, but for me it was mind-blowing.

Understanding that I can't control people, places and things – including Jimmy – but that I can only control my own actions and reactions was key. All our fights were stuffed with 'you' sentences: *you did this, you did that, you are this, you are that.* Therapy taught me that all conflict should focus on 'I' sentences: *I feel this, I heard this, I want this, I need this,* because all we can do is communicate our feelings and our needs and hope the other person is able and willing to listen.

In one of our final therapy sessions, our therapist said something that, to this day, remains the mantra of our relationship, and if you take nothing else away from reading this book, then I hope that this stays with you. I think I was wanging on about how he never put anything in the dishwasher and just left it on the counter right above the dishwasher. That, I was explaining, felt *worse* than if he'd just left it on the coffee table in the living room. Somehow, doing the easy bit and not taking a minute of his time to finish the task by either emptying the clean crockery to make room for his dirty plate or washing it up, or even just adding it to the dirty load that was already in there, felt like the ultimate 'fuck you'. He saw just a dirty plate that he'd had the good grace to take to the kitchen. I saw a big sign that said, 'That fucking bitch will do it.'

My therapist looked at me and I was expecting her to challenge me by saying something infuriating like, 'What's the fear around the dirty plate being left there?', but instead she simply said, 'You didn't feel very kept in mind.'

You didn't feel very kept in mind.

It wasn't a question. It was a statement of fact. It wasn't about what he'd done or said; it was about how the whole thing had made me feel. It didn't point to Jimmy or his faults, it didn't apportion blame. It wasn't angry or aggressive or manipulative. It simply stated clearly and honestly, in those few words, exactly how I felt every time Jimmy did something not very 'mental loady'. To this day, we will use that phrase, when something starts to niggle in the way only a resentment can, to explain calmly and without aggression or finger pointing that we don't feel good about something the other person has or has not done. When I come across that dirty plate these days, I won't shove it in the sink and furiously wash it, planning wild and wonderful ways to get rid of my husband without ending up in jail. Instead, I'll take a minute to cool my jets and then simply say something like, 'I didn't feel very kept in mind when I saw that dirty plate on the countertop.'

But here's the key – that needs to go both ways. *That* was the part that I was missing. I expected Jimmy to keep me in mind all the time, but I wasn't thinking at all about keeping him in mind. I was expecting Jimmy to change without having any expectations of changing myself. I didn't see it as a simultaneous process where we would both independently *at the same time* work towards being better versions of ourselves, together. I saw it as a 'you go first and then I'll consider it' thing. Jimmy understood that a lot more quickly than I did but, eventually, after another two years of therapy, we both got to a place where Frieda felt we were ready to go it alone and, honestly, we've never looked back.

I know it's frustrating when people talk about how therapy transformed their lives, but they don't *actually* tell you what they did on a practical level. I've tried my best to think of as many things that Jimmy and I tried to do consistently after therapy. I can't make any guarantees and it's really important you read these as things *you* need to do and not as things you think *your partner* should do.

Stop focusing on how shit the other person is
I am embarrassed to admit how much time and energy I spent thinking about and talking about how shit I thought Jimmy, and the way he behaved, was. I spent so much time complaining to my friends and family about his latest incompetence, his latest thoughtless act or mind-numbingly stupid decision that, actually, it's no wonder I always felt like I didn't have enough time to get on top of my list of things to do. Obviously, I only had those discussions with people who I knew would co-sign my bullshit. I wasn't about to set myself

up for a come-to-Jesus chat with someone who dared to point out that maybe, just maybe, I had played a part in all this.

Focus on your own shit behaviour, because that's the only thing you can change and put right
I resisted this strongly. I could only focus on the things that Jimmy did wrong and was totally blind to the idea that I had a part to play in the breakdown of our marriage. I didn't see my gossiping about Jimmy with my girlfriends as part of the problem. I saw it as a totally normal thing to do, a way to feel better about myself and my righteous anger. Post-therapy, I started to focus on the shit things I'd done or, at the very least, the questionable decisions I'd made or reactions I'd had or things I'd said. It took me years to learn that didn't mean that I was at fault, or taking the blame. I was just keeping my side of the street clean and apologising for any and all mistakes I made, be they central to the issue or not.

Stop treating each other like the enemy and start seeing each other as an ally
This was really hard for me, and it still is. I often have to take myself off after a tense conversation and actively remind myself that Jimmy loves me, he doesn't hate me, he's not out to get me or shame me or judge me. When I see Jimmy as the enemy, I am putting myself in the middle of everything. When I see him as an ally, I am putting the relationship in the middle of everything. It's hard and I'm not great at it, but it's progress not perfection and I'm trying. It's also important that you see 'fixing your relationship' as a team effort and not a solo

endeavour. Imagine you're playing doubles in tennis. If your partner hits a ball in the net you wouldn't scream and shout at them and tell them how shit they are. You'd look them in the eye and say, *Don't worry. We all fuck up. Let it go and move on.* Play more doubles.

Say you're sorry promptly

I hate saying I'm sorry and I guess most of you do too. There are very few people in this world who are totally comfortable with owning their part in things and apologising in a timely fashion. I've spent years bargaining with my conscience. To myself, I'd say things like, *I'll apologise when he does* or, *What he did was worse so he needs to apologise first* or, *Of course I behaved badly . . . anyone would if they were treated the way he treated me.* All of these ideas meant that I was saying my behaviour was conditionally reactive to his. Saying sorry felt like I was giving up my power or conceding defeat in some way, but I'd already given up my power well before that. I'd given up my power when I let his behaviour dictate my own. Saying sorry for your part in it, in an unconditional way, that doesn't relate at all to your partner's part in it, is the biggest act of power-snatching you can do. Trust me – I know. I've never felt like a worse human than when Jimmy is the first to apologise for his part in it, especially when I know that I've been the bigger dick.

Remember that an expectation is a resentment waiting to happen

Get acutely aware of those times when you are setting traps for your partner to fall into. It might be conscious, like the time I left the pile of stuff on the stairs and waited to see how long it would take him to pick it up and take it upstairs so that I could beat him over the head with it. Or, it might be less manipulative than that, more subconscious. Either way, I quickly figured out that stopping to say, 'I'm feeling a little resentful that you haven't taken your laundry upstairs. Would you mind doing that?' is a lot easier than setting traps and executing an evil plan of destruction just so that I can make the person I love feel shit about themselves. On the flip side, if you feel like you've fallen into a trap set up for you by your partner, don't explode. Sure, their behaviour has been shitty, but that doesn't mean yours needs to be.

Wait for your second (or third) thought
My default is generally 'lose shit and figure it out later'. It's a fight-or-flight response to those moments when I'm feeling attacked or at risk of being caught out. I try very hard these days to avoid reacting and try now to *respond* instead. I'd say I'm scoring 65 per cent success rate with this and that's after almost three years of really trying. In recovery there's an acronym that I found really helpful:

S – stop
O – observe
B – breathe
E – evaluate
R – respond

Just because it's hard doesn't mean it's wrong
It's really fucking hard – *all of this is really fucking hard* – and the only people who tell you it's easy are lying through their

perfect teeth or acting in a rom-com. No one else, no one *real*, has ever in the history of men and women hooking up together said that it's a walk in the park. So, if it's hard, it doesn't always mean that it's wrong. I remember once, in the middle of an argument, in a moment of total exasperation, I screamed in frustration and said, 'The thing is, this is really fucking hard. I'm finding this whole thing really hard.' Jimmy stopped immediately and looked at me, exhaled a huge sigh of relief and simply said, 'Me too.' And that was it. Sometimes, you just need to admit without fear of it meaning anything else that, right now, in the moment, it's just really bloody hard, and that's okay.

Don't gossip about your relationship
For the sake of clarity, I'm defining gossip as talking about someone when they're not in the room. There are times, of course, when you have to talk about other people in relation to yourself or something that's happened between you and that person but there are ways to do that respectfully and ways that are just gossiping. Banging on about your version of events with your girlfriends while you all drink wine is gossiping. Finding a close, trusted person and organising a time to have a confidential discussion about how to handle a situation is constructive. If the conversation you're having is designed to make yourself feel better about something or to get others to co-sign on your story, then it's gossip. If the conversation you're having is about identifying your part in something and finding a solution, that's constructive. Gossip is a very, very dangerous thing. I didn't realise how much gossip had played a part in the breakdown of so many of my

relationships, both romantic and platonic, until I got sober and realised how uncomfortable gossip feels when you're focusing on your part in things.

It's even more important when it comes to your marriage. If you're saying stuff to your mates that you haven't said clearly and kindly to your husband, then you're part of the problem and not part of the solution.

Get into the habit of communicating about everything
You know when you have that enormous row, the one that's been brewing for weeks? You've both known it's coming and, as the days have gone on and the resentments have grown, you've been quietly arming yourself with a defence worthy of an appearance at the Old Bailey. Then, when it finally happens and you both press the fuck-it button on your anger, you get it all out in a messy, dramatic and exhausting argument that probably ends with one of you storming out. Or maybe you plough on through, determined to get to the other side of this argument no matter the cost. Either way, there's only two ways an argument can end – reconciliation or divorce.

Jimmy and I used to have those kind of fights and, eventually, reconciliation would come, but only after we'd tuckered ourselves out screaming. Like toddlers in a tantrum, we would suddenly just run out of steam and start to talk quietly, often because we simply didn't have the energy to shout anymore. Inevitably, we'd finally start listening to each other and lo and behold we'd figure it out. Pride, stubbornness, fear, rage – all of these things had got in the way, and when we'd used them all up, we were able to get to the root of the issue. There was always that moment when we'd finally understand what each other had been trying to say the whole time.

When we came out of therapy, we got into the habit of talking about something *as soon as it bothered us* and, let me tell you, it was so fucking boring. Initially we spent all day, every day just talking about the things that made us feel resentful. I think we must have told each other we didn't feel particularly kept in mind a hundred times a day. But, as time went on, we found ourselves talking less about the things that annoyed us about each other and more about something we saw in the news or something funny that happened to us on the tube.

To this day, we still bring things up as soon as they happen. Just this morning I told Jimmy I was feeling resentful that he never put the oil and vinegar bottles away properly and it was annoying because it made it harder to clean around them. He nodded and said, 'Got it. I'll do better.' A few days ago, he told me he was feeling resentful about something I'd said to a friend of ours. Of course, my first instinct was to defend myself and tell him I was only joking or that he shouldn't take himself too seriously, but I stopped, observed, breathed, evaluated and then responded with, 'I hear you. I'm sorry I made you feel that way.'

I know, I know. I can hear the roll of a million eyes (hopefully!) as you read this. Yes, we are those people. We are that infuriating couple who actually bloody work things through. We avoid way more arguments than we have and I'm more than a little aware of how smug this can make me sound ... and as I've built a brand on being @notsosmugnow, it's more than a little off-brand. But, it's also something I'm incredibly proud of. It's been a long, expensive, painful and exhausting slog, but we both dug deep, every day, to hold our relationship safely and carry it to where it is now. Here's the crap news: I've realised there's no finish line when it comes to working on your marriage. Instead, there's a new starting line every day; the race starts afresh and you both have to decide to keep running.

14

I'm the Problem, It's Me

'The world is changed by your example, not your opinion' – Paulo Coelho, *The Alchemist*

I suppose at this point in the book, you might be thinking, *Huh, this book isn't what I thought it was going to be.* Maybe you thought this was going to be a book about the war stories of my marriage, a literary car crash that you can drive by slowly looking out for the guts and gore dripping onto the highway of married life so that you can temporarily feel a bit better about your own situation.

Alternatively, maybe you were looking for a book that spends 80,000 words banging on about how awful men are. If that's the case, you may be a little disappointed by now. Yes, my husband can be woefully inept when it comes to navigating what I think are very basic domestic tasks, but I've come to realise that bitching and moaning about him may make me feel better temporarily, but it's not fixing anything.

Of course, the mishandling of the mental load isn't all my fault; it's not even mostly my fault. I wasn't the only one getting shit wrong all the time in my marriage. Trust me.

Jimmy was responsible for some monumental fuck-ups too. His communication was dire in a different way. While I was the martyr, doing everything for everyone and then making them all feel terrible about it, he was a chronic people-pleaser. He put everyone else's needs and feelings before his own and pretended everything was fine because the thought of confrontation or conflict in any way, shape or form terrified him. This basically meant I'd behave badly, he'd roll over and take it, and neither of us had *actually* been honest about what we were feeling. Ever.

But, this is my book and not his, and so I can really only tell my story, not his. I can make some guesses and talk about how his behaviour and choices *felt* to me as one of the people experiencing the consequences of that behaviour and those choices, but when it comes to changing for the better, when it comes to actually making a difference to our relationship and its dynamic, I can only change myself, and so throughout this book, I'm focusing on my part in it.

I could sit here and write a whole book about what I thought Jimmy did wrong in our relationship. Really. It might even have two or three volumes(!), but it would be a pointless exercise because I can't change a damn thing about him. I can make my own feelings clear in an honest way rather than a manipulative way (easier said than done for me), but really, what I've come to believe is true is this: the only way to encourage change in another is through attraction and not promotion. So, if I change myself and my dastardly ways and just focus on keeping my side of the street clean, somehow the idea is that, magically, Jimmy will rise up to meet me and change his way of handling things as well. They say nothing changes if nothing changes and that couldn't be more true, but they also say you can't control people, places and things, you can only control your own actions and reactions, so the change had to start with me.

In reality, because he's a much better human than I am, the change started with Jimmy. Between us, he was the first to seriously change his behaviour. How and why that happened isn't my story to tell, but I suddenly noticed he was taking responsibility for his part in things when they went wrong. Our traditional MO was to have a very dramatic fight with tears, screaming, vicious insults and dramatic exits. At some point, he would leave, as usual, but unusually he started coming back more quickly and saying weird things like, 'Look, I've thought about my part in it and I realise I *insert his part in it here* and I'm sorry.' Let me tell you, if you're used to going head to head, to the death, in a marital fight, it's really fucking confronting when one of you suddenly turns around and says they're sorry for their part in it.

It actually made me mad at first. I thought he was doing it to make me look and feel bad. My level of self-centredness was, quite clearly, off the scale. It was, embarrassingly, unfathomable to me that someone would take themselves off to calmly and rationally think about the conflict and return quickly to apologise for their part in it with no agenda or expectation of an apology in return. While Jimmy stormed off, I usually used that time to talk to myself and justify my feelings of rage. I'd have a pity-party dressed up as a courtroom drama where Jimmy had no defence and was always found guilty. The difference was that I would direct my energy towards Jimmy and all the things he did wrong without taking a moment to point that same energy towards myself to consider that I may have an apology or two to make as well.

Of course, once he'd delivered his apology, it would leave a gaping chasm of silence where my apology was supposed to go because, no matter how you spin it, if there's two of you fighting, then there's two apologies required. It doesn't matter about who's right and who's wrong, and it took me a mortifyingly long time to realise that. It's about how it's handled, and if we're both shouting and screaming at each other, then we've both fucked up. Eventually, I would, reluctantly and begrudgingly, start to apologise in return. It was deeply, deeply uncomfortable for me. It still is.

I grew up in a house where no one apologised, where the person who could argue the most effectively won and where being right was the only end goal. Kindness, accommodation, acceptance – none of these things got a look-in because we all lived and breathed pride and ego. To apologise was to admit you were wrong and to admit you were wrong was a weakness of the most shameful and embarrassing kind. My family weren't like this because they were horrible human beings; they were like this because they were hurt human beings. Their stories aren't mine to tell and there's nothing exceptional about their experiences but none of us get through this life unscathed and my family weren't any different.

To this day, apologising to my husband is the hardest thing I have to do and I'm ashamed to admit that, nine times out of ten, he's still the one to apologise first, but the point of this is to say that, against all the odds, I rose up to meet him, not because he demanded it of me, but because his change of behaviour was, at first, curious to me and, eventually, attractive to me. I began to see that my apology didn't depend on his and vice versa. He could still technically be 'wrong'. Maybe he did piss all over the floor, or miss another doctor's appointment for our kids, but chances are, my reaction required an apology, because unless I said, 'Dude, it's okay. I get it. We all fuck up, but I need you to do better at keeping me in mind in the future,' then I owed him an apology.

I think slowly, over time, the bar gets really low when it comes to the acceptability of how we treat our partners. Of course it does. We see them all the time. We interact with them all the time. Sometimes it's hard to see where we end and they begin. We have been through the trenches with them. We have seen each other at our worst but that emotional comfort can mean we can start to take liberties with their hearts and souls. We will say things to them that we would never dare utter to another human being. We will treat them in a way that no one else in our lives would accept – and it goes both ways, right?

I used to say to Jimmy, 'I want the Jimmy that everyone else gets,' because we would go out and he would be charming and funny and cheeky and everyone would spend the night telling me how wonderful he was. I'd nod and agree, but as soon as we got back home, he'd be grumpy, distant and snappy with me, and I know Jimmy felt the same way about me. Despite us loving each other, and recognising each other as our person, we somehow forgot to treat each other that way. If he was the most special person in my life – why was I more worried about how I treated the man in the post office than I was about how I treated him?*

What has this all got to do with the mental load? Firstly, it's a damn sight more stressful to manage the mental load when you don't feel like the people you live with are on your team. Resentments spring up like whack-a-mole when the people you're looking after treat you badly. Secondly, on the flip side, the people you live with are far more reluctant to put themselves in your Cinderella shoes if you're always communicating valid points in a bitchy way. And finally, the real message of the mental load and how it feels to carry it tends to get lost when you're screaming and shouting because you're at the end of your tether and bringing in – whether you know it or not – a load of other residual resentments and traumas.

Learning to catch myself before I made unwise decisions or said hurtful things was probably the most difficult part of my transition into a reasonable human being. Lashing out and hitting back had become an instinct that, for many years, I'd resorted to when the fear of making a mistake, and therefore making myself completely unlovable, was dragged to the surface. I never thought to look for a reason why I would sometimes behave so badly, even though I hated myself for doing it. Instead, I would resort to my tried-and-tested theory that I was, actually, just a shit human. It never occurred to me that somehow I'd conflated perfection with lovability and that the fear of being unlovable, unwanted or unacceptable was at the root of all my reactive behaviour.

---

* Sidenote: that's probably not a great comparison, mostly because I hate the post office and I *may* have been known to behave pretty badly there too.

It wasn't *just* trauma or adverse experiences that were responsible for my questionable behaviour. As a woman, I'm also riddled with hormones, and while I will never use that as an excuse when they play the showreel of my worst bits, I gently and humbly offer it up as an explanation for some of the times I overreacted, lost my shit or burst into tears and blamed everyone else. As I've got older and closer to the menopause, the role that my hormones play in my ability to function as a reasonable human being in this world has come into sharp focus. As I watch my daughters barrel towards puberty, I see the possessive way in which their hormones grab hold of them, lock-jawed, and turn them into feral versions of themselves. While these hormonal shifts may not be our fault, I have come to understand that they are ours to manage. I'm not absolving our male counterparts from considering our cycles, or expressing empathy and support, but we have to meet them halfway. Easier said than done, girls, I know. Easier said than done.

15

Hormoaning

'There are only two mammals who have evolved to survive after their childbearing years: toothed whales and humans.'
– Dr Jen Gunter, OB/GYN and author of *The Menopause Manifesto: Own Your Health with Facts and Feminism*

At the time of writing, I am forty-three, and in the last few months, I have once again felt the blindsiding impact of my hormones on my mental health and physical capabilities. The first time I felt a huge hormonal shift was when I was in my early teens – and then of course it happened monthly until I fell pregnant. With my two pregnancies and postnatal phases came a whole different set of hormonal shifts that turned me inside out emotionally. Now, eight years later, the perimenopause just asked my ADHD to hold its beer.

My first period was pretty traumatic. I don't really remember much from my childhood but I do remember the feeling of a big, cumbersome pad between my legs for the first time. I remember the crippling anxiety that came with being expected to walk around like I wasn't bleeding continuously from between my legs – plus, at that time, there was still a lot of shame and secrecy around periods. It was a deeply distressing time for me and one I still look back on with sadness.

At the time, I was playing a lot of tennis and my parents had paid for me and my best friend to have private tennis coaching twice a week. My period started on a day I was supposed to be going to tennis. I felt awful. I felt sick and icky and was fraught with discomfort on a physical and emotional level. I remember being disgusted by the feeling of blood bubbling out of me and pushing its way between my labia to land (hopefully!) on the pad. To this day, I still struggle with that sensation.

I begged my mum not to make me go to the lesson. The last thing I wanted to do was wear a white skirt and white knickers and run around chasing after balls with a sanitary pad the size of a brick wedged up against my vulva. I just wanted to sit in the bath for hours and then lie in bed with a hot-water bottle and a level of privacy that meant I didn't have to worry about whether I'd leaked through my clothes. But, ever the victim of social expectations of women, my mother made me go, telling me that the world didn't stop for my period. That I had to carry on as normal because this was how life was now.

My mum believed she was doing the right thing, and honestly, maybe she was. We'll never know, but what I do know is that she didn't tell me to do that because her motherly instincts thought it was for the best. She did it because she knew that we lived, and still live, in a world where women's hormones, their physical changes and their bleeding, are absolutely not accommodated. Instead, these things are reviled, chained to shame and disgust and, in my mother's mind, sending me out to sink or swim in the menstrual flow was about building up an armour to exist in a world that didn't give a shit about me or my period. The patriarchy, after all, waits for no menstrual cycle, and a game of tennis was going to seem like a walk in the park when I discovered what it was like to be a grown-up with grown-up periods and grown-up responsibilities.

There are, of course, times when I think we should encourage our children to push through when they don't want to do something. If they've committed to a term's worth of football lessons, for example, they should (in my opinion) finish the term. After that, if they want to drop it, that's okay. But when my daughters start their periods, I'm not going to force them to do anything they don't feel like doing. There will be plenty of time for them to 'woman up', but the first day of their first period is, in my opinion, not the occasion.

Instead, I truly, truly believe that when a girl starts her period we should be nothing but gentle with her. We should cocoon her, make her feel safe, encourage her to check in with herself and her body, really connect with how she's feeling and learn to respond accordingly. I was taught to ignore pain, to pretend I was a pair of curtains and pull myself together. I was taught that we carry on regardless. Yes, her period and the accompanying hormones are something she's going to have to deal with for the rest of her fertile life, but that doesn't mean we have to teach her how to do it baptism-of-fire style.

As a perimenopausal woman, I have been rudely reminded of how discombobulating a significant hormonal shift can be. I'm a woman in my forties and I am struggling to cope with it, so imagine a teenage girl, dealing with it for the first time, at a moment when the world feels so cold and cruel and she is so very breakable. Strength isn't just there, inherent within us all. It needs nurturing and building up; facing the world on the world's terms while you're on your period is no mean feat. It's hard and testing and painful and I think we are often guilty of underestimating the impact it can have on our tweens and teens.

Teaching girls to mask what's really going on for them is also part of the bigger problem and relates perfectly to the mental load. Throughout our childhood and adolescence, girls quickly learn that making a fuss about the fact that our uterus is painfully shedding its skin is never well-received and rarely elicits anything close to sympathy. Periods, it seems, are to be neither seen, nor heard. *We are women!* our foremothers declared. *We don't give in to pain, we don't speak up, we don't question it, we don't talk about it. We keep calm and carry on and, most importantly, we keep it to ourselves.*

The idea that you carry on as normal, as a young girl, when you start your first period is a perfect example of how we are taught that society is never going to make space for our differences. And so, we mask the painful cramps. We swallow the anxiety around leaking that every woman, every day of her bleeding life, feels. We walk tall when what we really want to do is lie in the foetal position with a hot-water bottle and a never-ending supply of ibuprofen. We put a smile on our face when it feels like our uterus has grown spikes. We watch our mothers take care of everyone and even though, with every sigh and huff, we suspect they're not entirely okay, we can't help but notice that, invariably, they stay silent. *Huh,* we think to ourselves, *I guess women don't speak up when they're feeling upset or unappreciated.* And that's the lesson we take with us when our own lives and experiences turn into 'same, same but different' versions of our mothers' later in life.

Hormones weren't the only thing that I masked on an Oscar-winning level. When I was forty, I was diagnosed with ADHD. I know, I know. It does seem like *everyone* has ADHD at the moment, but for me it was a tricky process coming to terms with a diagnosis late in life. At first, I was flooded with relief. *I'm not useless or broken*, I thought. It's not my fault that I find seemingly simple and straightforward tasks difficult, or that I consistently miss appointments, or that my forgetfulness and absent-mindedness cause me to question whether I have early-onset dementia.

Then came the anger, hitting me like a truck. Every time I'd been screamed at in primary school for forgetting my maths homework, missing a music lesson or not having my PE kit suddenly felt so painfully unfair. At university, my tutor had threatened to kick me off my course in my first year because he caught me plagiarising an essay. This had confounded me, because it was so unlike me to do something like that. But because I simply couldn't manage my time, my schedules and my workload, I'd panicked and copied parts of an essay I'd found online. Once I was diagnosed, I understood what had led me to make that fateful decision, a decision about which I'd felt so much shame that I never told anyone . . . until now. There were hundreds of moments, decisions, actions that I'd struggled to understand and then suddenly, here was the reason – ADHD. I was furious that no one had ever asked, *'How can we support you here?'* and instead had just shouted at me and shamed me.

After the anger, came sadness. Sadness for the little girl who hadn't had a brother or sister to whisper the questions she needed answers to in the middle of the night. Sadness for the little girl who stood in a school corridor, desperately trying not to cry when her headmaster shouted in her face so loudly that her hair blew back a little with the force of it. The little girl who tried to ignore the fact that the doors to all the classrooms on the corridor were open and everyone could hear. The not-so-little girl who struggled in social situations and found that alcohol helped her be who she needed to be.

By my early twenties, I had perfected the art of masking the symptoms of my ADHD that I thought at the time were evidence that I was a pretty useless human. I had enough evidence at this point to understand that my natural state of being was faulty. It always seemed to get me into trouble and so I became fastidious about my belongings and where they went. If anything was out of place, I'd be furious, anxious and terrified all at once. I knew I couldn't afford to lose any of my possessions because all experiential evidence up to that point showed me that I would probably be shouted at if I were to do so. I began arriving at appointments and meetings embarrassingly early. If I had to catch a flight at 9pm, I'd be at the airport at 9am. Once I was with Jimmy, it was me who decided when we needed to leave the house to be somewhere, which became a huge point of contention. He couldn't under-stand why I'd need to allow two hours to travel six stops on the Jubilee line. I couldn't understand why he couldn't under-stand it. I rushed everywhere. I did everything at a million miles a minute. I made a spreadsheet for everything and spent a fortune on lever-arch folders to ensure I didn't lose another piece of paper ever again.

It may sound like, in some ways, I just got my shit together. But, the effort it took me, with my ADHD-addled brain, to achieve these things was astronomical, and when I was twenty-six, I suffered my first ADHD burnout. Of course, no one called it that. No one even considered that I had ADHD. As I described earlier, they just called it depression and put me on Prozac. I took Prozac for a year, weaned myself off it, felt fine and then, two years later, the same thing happened again. Until I was diagnosed at forty, I believed I struggled with depression and occasionally required anti-depressants.

When the psychiatrist, who was assessing me for ADHD, asked me to describe how those depressive episodes presented themselves, I told him.

'I would collapse, physically on the floor. It was like I couldn't do anything anymore. I'd be crying hysterically and then just ball up in the foetal position and almost go into a trance-like state.'

It happened once when I was living with Jimmy. I remember lying on the floor in our hallway, repeating 'I just can't do it anymore' over and over. Looking back, it never felt like I imagined depression to feel, and I think I knew, on some level, that it wasn't depression. But when doctors are telling you that you have depression, you believe them. Instead, it felt like my brain had been firing on all cylinders for so long that it had started misfiring and then suddenly, the fuse had blown. The whole system just shut down. I don't remember Jimmy helping me up and putting me to bed, but when I woke up almost twenty-four hours later, I went back on to anti-depressants and the whole cycle started again.

When I was officially diagnosed at forty, my psychiatrist explained that it sounded like ADHD burnout and not a depressive episode. He said it was particularly common in women who hadn't been diagnosed and had been furiously masking symptoms for a problem they had no idea existed. 'ADHD,' he said, 'is manageable, but you can't be expected to manage something you don't know you have.' I burst into tears and experienced the relief→anger→sadness cycle all over again.

The same applies to our hormones. Science hasn't prioritised investigating the female body, its hormones and the consequences of them. Instead, women have been given the bare bones when it comes to understanding how our body works and even then, only in relation to the parts that affect the baby-making bits. I was in my thirties before I knew what my vulva was. I'd always referred to it as my vagina. I had no idea the vagina was internal and the vulva was the external part that could be seen. The recent increase in discussions around perimenopause and menopause aren't happening because the symptoms of the menopause are suddenly getting worse. They're happening because *they have never happened before*. The time we live in – the twenty-first century – is the *first* time any real efforts have been made to fully understand what happens to a woman's body and mind when the menopause kicks in and the *first* time there has been space to talk about it openly.

Because of the ignorance surrounding the physiological effects of women's hormones, we have been taught that women are just overly emotional or irrational or a bit useless. And, even though we were never allowed to use our hormonal shifts as an excuse for *anything,* especially if we were going to keep 'banging on' about equality, men didn't hesitate to weaponise those very same 'not real' hormones against us for their own gain. Questions like, *Are you due on?* or *Feeling a bit hormonal, are we?* have been used by men against women to deflect from their own fuck-ups for millennia. It's some of the most impressively constructed gaslighting the world has ever seen. Keyser Söze got it wrong when he said, 'The greatest trick the Devil ever pulled was convincing the world he didn't exist.' No. The greatest trick ever pulled was men convincing women that our hormones didn't exist and that what we were feeling wasn't biological, it was just bitchy, and even though we knew, quite literally in our waters, that they were wrong, we didn't have a chance in hell of winning that battle.

But here we are, one of only two species in the world in which the female has evolved to live beyond her fertile years. Let's be really clear about this – it's wild. It's also interesting that men have not evolved to live beyond their fertile years. Sure, they are fertile for longer, but I'd bet both my ovaries that if men became infertile around the same age as women do, they wouldn't have evolved to live for much longer. Why? Because, when we get down to the fundamentals of what's necessary for existence, what fucking use are they? Honestly, in the grand scheme of things, once they are too old to hunt and gather, what's the point of men if they can't inseminate women?

On the other hand, women live. They continue to live well beyond their childbearing years, and that's significant. It's significant because nothing in nature happens by accident. In many ways, the world would be a better place with fewer humans in it, so why are we kept around? I'll tell you why *I* think we're kept around – because on a logistical and emotional level, the human species wouldn't be able to exist without women, and this, *this* is probably why we magnetically attract the mental load. Because when it comes down to it, men and children need looking after. And when those children have their own children, they need someone to show them how to look after those children, because it's not as if the men are going to do it, is it?

Something has gone very, very wrong, though. Somehow, somewhere along the lines of time, our evolutionary destiny has got its wires crossed with the day-to-day running of a family and household. We, the female of the species, are supposed to be the guardians of the species. But, existing as we do, in a society dominated by men, we have also become the guardians of the laundry, the cleaning, the lists, the present-buying and the appointment-making. I think we're only just waking up to the reality that, in this case, 1+1 does not equal 2.

16

The Shit-Sandwich Generation

'A hero is an ordinary individual who finds the strength
to persevere and endure in spite of overwhelming obstacles.'
– Christopher Reeve

The term 'sandwich generation' may feel like a shiny new phrase
that social media invented to describe a fairly new phenomenon,
but don't be deceived. The term is actually as old as me. It was
coined in 1981 by Dorothy Miller and Elaine Brody, two social
workers, who first conceptualised the pressure felt by a generation of people who found themselves looking after small
children and elderly parents at the same time. It's a recent
sociological shift that is the result of longer life spans and
women having children later in life. There are loads of statistics
about how many people make up the sandwich generation,
but essentially these are the highlights: more and more of us
are finding ourselves part of this club (sandwich . . . sorry I
couldn't resist) that we never asked to be in and – try not to
die of shock – it's an issue that affects mostly men. Only joking!
Of course, it's an issue that affects mostly women.

The concept of the sandwich generation is something that

I am personally experiencing in real time. I've previously mentioned the Newborn version of the mental load. Well this is the Sandwich version. This is a brand-new tentacle to the list of things we have to worry about that, in my experience, emerged just as my kids were happily settled in school and I was starting to feel the pressure ease a little. Typical. I should have known not to rest on my laurels.

About seven years ago, my mum was diagnosed with Parkinson's disease, and in the last two years, her decline has been rapid. Do you know what the cruellest thing about Parkinson's is, though? It isn't the shakes, or the memory loss. No – those things are horrible, but the worst thing about this disease is that it *doesn't* kill you. It just steals your body and your functions from you and, if you're lucky, it will also take your mind. I say 'lucky' because Parkinson's is brutal, and if you can endure the final stages with very little awareness of what's going on then I think, in a lot of ways, that must be a blessing. Half of people with Parkinson's disease will develop dementia.

My mum is currently classified as Stage 5, which, spoiler alert, is the final stage. Of course, she could live for another ten or fifteen years, or she could pass away tomorrow from something totally unrelated. She requires full-time care, which my dad has taken on with a kindness and enthusiasm that has impressed us all and for which we are all grateful. But he is eighty-two, and while he's mentally fit as a really annoying, slightly right-wing fiddle, physically, he's kind of falling apart. He'll take serious umbrage with that description of himself and remind me that he still goes to the gym two or three times a week. But, that's only possible because he's had a new knee and a new hip fitted in the last three years. His hands are riddled with arthritis and despite the bits and pieces that have been replaced, he walks slowly and hunched. He's fine and, God willing, he'll be around to annoy the shit out of me for a few years yet, but as much as he'd hate to admit it, he's also vulnerable.

Did I mention my parents also live in Devon, which is exactly 184.9 miles away from where I live? With some luck and a good wind, I can drive there in about 3.5 hours, but mostly, it takes 4 hours or costs about £100 for a return train ticket. That's a lot of time and money to take into account before I've even got to their front door, and being with them means that I have to leave my kids and husband behind.

Currently, my responsibility to my parents isn't as intense as it could be or as it may turn out to be in the near future. We have people that come in and help my dad, and day to day they are able to manage. My role is to be constantly available on the end of the phone, to go down to Devon in an emergency or to simply give my dad some support. I try to be there for most hospital appointments and I spend a lot of time talking to Dad about next steps and plans for the future. Not that it's easy or even possible to make plans. Parkinson's is a cunning and baffling disease. It presents differently in everyone, its intensity varies and there's no prognosis because no one really knows how or when it's going to develop. Both Dad and I have a burning desire to put systems in place and plan for the future, but the disease doesn't really allow that and so we both spend a lot of time feeling as if we are fighting fires. For that reason, it's something that's always front and centre in my mind, and that's exhausting and emotionally very, very difficult.

If, like me, you're bearing the brunt of a fairly standard mental load as a woman in a family of four (and by 'standard' I mean 'brutal'), only to discover one day that you have to add in the responsibility of looking after your parents (who don't live down the road and who sometimes don't respond positively to that help), it can be enough to break you completely. It's not that we don't want to do it. Being able to be there for my parents and especially my mum has been a real privilege and a gift that I will treasure for ever.

It's also felt like a chance to repay my mum for all the things she did for me, things that I took for granted for so long but things that having my own children has helped me see and understand. I have a compassion for my mum that I could never have felt before having kids because I see now where a lot of her anger and sadness came from. At the time I would be frustrated with her and wonder why she couldn't just be happy with her life – it looked pretty good from where I was standing – but I understand now what it feels like to bear the mental load of a family and not feel seen or heard or appreciated. What I used to think was just nastiness, or a lack of gratitude, or self-pity, I now see as real pain and loneliness. I have come to accept my part in adding to the pain and loneliness she felt – I wasn't always very nice to my mum – but I was also just a child. So, while there are times that I may resent the added load of looking after my parents, there are also times when I am grateful to be able to be of service to them. It's not easy to manage those feelings but

I've come to know with certainty that two conflicting feelings can be true at the same time.

I can love my kids but not love the job of motherhood. I can love my parents but be angry that they didn't prepare properly for old age. I can want to help look after them while also hate leaving my husband and kids. I can want my mum to live for ever but also find myself hoping that she died peacefully in her sleep last night because, honestly, she deserves so much more than this. Hers isn't my story to tell, but I know the adversity she faced as a young adult, the strength she had to find to survive, and it breaks my heart that this is what her final years look like. After a lifetime of graft and giving, she should be enjoying doing the crossword every morning with a cup of coffee she can drink without help. She should be able to go and play mahjong with the other ladies in the village. She should be travelling, lunching with her friends, going on hiking holidays and enjoying her grand-children. Neither she, nor Dad, deserve this ending, and when I think about that, it always causes the emotional fault lines in my soul to shift. These oppositional feelings are not easy to deal with, but I've learned that accepting they are real and allowing myself to feel them all has been key to letting resentments go.

One thing I am incredibly grateful for is that I was called up to sandwich service *after* Jimmy and I had worked out the catastrophic kinks in our relationship (and I'm not talking about the fun, sexual kinks). By the time it became clear that I was going to have to split my time between Devon and London, Jimmy and I had done the therapy, we were both working on ourselves independently and we were working from the same playbook. So, Jimmy was able to say, 'I've got this. Whenever you need to go, just go,' and I didn't have to make lists about where the kids needed to go and when and what they needed to take with them. We'd addressed the balance already. Not only did that make it logistically easier, but it also allowed me to open up my heart to Jimmy even more, to love him more completely, to trust him with the most vulnerable parts of me.

So, while my time spent sandwiching has been really fucking hard – yes – I've also felt really supported, which, unsurprisingly, has made *all the difference*. No one else can do the sandwiching – that's all on me – so, instead, Jimmy took on my roles at home and we were both respectful of the fact that it was hard for everyone involved. Back in the olden days, we would have made it into some sadistic competition about who has it harder and who's more miserable and who's the bigger person. Now, we speak up about the resentments we have, knowing that they may not always be reasonable but that they must be aired nonetheless.

'I know I'm away and you're doing all the stuff at home,' I may venture, 'but I can't keep coming home to piles and piles of laundry. Can you try to do some while I'm away?'

Or Jimmy may say, 'You've been away so much recently but when you're home, you're also out and about all the time. I feel like I haven't had a chance to get some space.'

It would be easy for Jimmy to snap back with something along the lines of, 'I'm doing my best – you're the one that's away all the time,' or for me to retort, 'I may be home but I've still got to go out to work, you know?' It's taken us years to resist these reflexes and, of course, we're not always 100 per cent successful, but we are religious about making space for each other's resentments with a promise to not take it personally.

So while Jimmy stepped up, I also had to actively step down a bit. I had to accept that if he was going to be running the show at home, then I had to let him do it his way. Of course, that didn't stop me throwing a few 'constructive criticisms' his way, some of which he listened to and some of which he wilfully ignored, but in general, I had to accept that not everything could be perfect all at the same time. There's a saying that goes, 'The house can be perfect, the kids can be perfect, or I can be perfect, but you can't have all three.' Truer words have never been uttered.

But I know that, when it comes to this situation, in some ways, I'm a unicorn. I know that this isn't the lived experience of many, many women who find themselves stuck in the middle with an unsupportive partner while there are, as Stealers Wheel said, clowns to the left of me (kids), jokers to the right (parents). I have seen far stronger marriages than mine crumble under the pressure of an overloaded shit-sandwich, and this problem isn't going anywhere. In fact, it's only going to become more pronounced, because we're having kids later and living longer. My advice? If you're not part of the sandwich generation yet, now would be a really great time to start thinking about a plan for when you are. Don't do what we did and be wildly unaware of the freight train heading our way, dumping a few more shipping containers of mental load madness down on top of us.

While having to incorporate the care of your parents into your already burgeoning mental load will stretch you physically, financially and logistically, it'll also be a really difficult time for you emotionally. Unless you had an idyllic childhood which contained no trauma whatsoever and your parents are just the loveliest humans on the planet, then re-entering the parent/child dynamic in your forties is going to bring some shit to the surface – for you and them – and managing that is a whole emotional load of its own.

It's important to recognise that, in many cases, it's not the *physical act* of having to do all the stuff that sends women stratospherically crazy with stress; it's, more often than not, the constant *thinking* about having to do all those things. So when your intellectual brain is already running at a million miles a minute keeping track of the mental load (which, by the way, just increased tenfold with the introduction of caring for your parents) and then your subconscious brain gets kicked in the nuts with some trauma that you haven't worked out properly, triggered by your dad treating you like a fourteen-year-old or your mum shouting at you even though you're a grown-ass woman, then, chances are, you're not going to deal with that in an optimal way. Running around like a lunatic, trying to look after everyone is exhausting, but dealing with the sudden onslaught of mental and emotional pain that you've kept successfully locked in a box in the attic of your brain for a couple of decades? That's going to cut your spiritual legs off at the knees if you're not careful.

I went through a lot of arguments with my dad, tearful conversations with my husband and sleepless nights trying to do what I thought was best for my parents. It was turning myself inside out researching council websites, charity websites, NHS websites. I was coming up with suggestions and plans and inevitably, it would always end in a fight with my dad. It also meant I was taking on way more than I could possibly handle and so my mental health tanked. I talked to a friend and she asked me one simple question that blew my mind: *Did they ask you to do that?* Well no, I stuttered in response, but they need all the help they can get. *Sometimes*, she continued, *you need to give people the grace to make their own mistakes and the space to ask for help when they need it.* I spat out some sarcastic comment about how it would be a cold day in hell before my dad asked for help, but she encouraged me to try a different approach and see what happened.

From that point on, my mantras, when it came to dealing with my parents, were: *I support your decision* and *I'm here if you need help.* I used to bang on and on to Jimmy about how I didn't need him to 'fix' things for me, I just needed him to let me vent about whatever it was I had going on. I realised that, unwittingly, I'd been guilty of doing the same thing to my parents. Helping, I've learned, isn't about doing it all, or controlling it all. Sometimes, it's just about being there, being humble, being quiet and being available. I'm not great at that but, out of necessity, I've had to learn to try because, in the simplest of terms, I *can't* fucking do it all. And, just like that, the mental load that came with caring for my parents was reduced significantly.

This was just another example of how I was, in some cases, responsible for exacerbating my own mental load. I wasn't doing it on purpose. It's not like I got off on taking myself by the hand and leading myself towards a mental breakdown. But, women have been bred, since the dawn of time, to care for the people around us. Much like generational trauma, there is a generational sense of responsibility that has been passed down, almost on a genetic level, to each and every one of us. We don't even know we're doing it, but I'm going to take this opportunity to gently suggest that each and every one of us gets uncomfortably honest about whether we are actually getting in our own way.

17

Handling Your Balls

'Most of us have trouble juggling. The woman who says
she doesn't is someone I admire but have never met.'
– Barbara Walters

Warning: I'm going to use the word 'balls' a lot in this chapter.
I once made an analogy online about the balls we juggle
(no, not those balls) and I referred to it as *the juggle struggle*.
Of course, it's just another way to describe the mental load
– each ball is an item on our 'to-do' list – but the image
of a woman juggling all the balls and doing all she can to
ensure she doesn't drop any was a visual that everyone
seemed to relate to. I can't imagine that I coined the phrase,
but I certainly hadn't heard it before and it seemed to
encapsulate perfectly what life as a mum, a wife, a business
owner, a daughter, a friend, and all the other roles we play,
felt like.

There are just so many balls and the reality is, no matter
how hard we try, we don't have enough hands to keep them
all in the air at once. Forget what we're told about having it
all and doing it all. I hope by now you've read enough in

this book to feel like you've finally been given a pass on living up to that expectation. It is simply impossible to not drop a ball here or there.

So what if, and hear me out here, we *acknowledge* and *accept* the fact that it's an impossible task? What would it feel like to lean in and be clear about the fact that those balls are not going to keep themselves in the air so someone else is going to have to handle a few balls or we are going to have to get comfortable with dropping a few? Or we could consciously put a few balls down?

It's easy to say, but I know it's not easy to do. I'm a ball hoarder. I don't like to put balls down and I definitely don't like dropping them. In fact, I'm not even sure I know how to put balls down. In my mind, they aren't always individual balls. Instead, it's one massive 'mental load' ball that I'm carrying, valiantly, on my shoulders, like Atlas bearing the weight of the globe. Maybe it's because, as a child, I was always rewarded for achievement – for doing something exceptional. Love wasn't necessarily shown through cuddly chats and movie nights on the sofa. Love was shown when I aced an exam or won a gold medal at a swimming gala – being the best at something was valued highly and so, when it comes to juggling the balls of the mental load, I am always acutely aware that dropping balls does not a gold medal win and, therefore, doesn't get me noticed and loved.

What if all balls are not created equal, though? What if some balls are big and some are smaller? What if some are heavier and some lighter? What if some are glass and some are plastic? It's not a concept I came up with – I can't remember where I heard it – but the idea that we can choose which balls to juggle based on our capacity at any given time blew my mind.

When you start to see all the balls as different and individual in their own right, you can start to understand that the juggle doesn't have to be such a struggle. The glass balls are balls that, obviously, need to be protected at all times. Dropping the glass balls can have serious consequences, so of course those need to be prioritised. They are things like paying your bills, turning up at work, looking after your health, your kids' wellbeing, taking accountability, practising an attitude of gratitude, getting enough sleep. What surprised me – and maybe it will surprise you too – was that the glass balls weren't actually things I furiously scribbled down on my to-do list with an inexplicable sense of urgency. Apart from paying my bills, the glass balls were all everyday behaviours that I needed to make sure were the foundation of any actions I needed to take. There may be times when these are the only balls you can handle – and I've had to learn that's okay.

Take right now, for instance. I'm currently writing this book. It's a mammoth task and one that I'm thoroughly enjoying, but also one that is causing me some anxiety. I want this book to be the best I can make it, but I am on a tight deadline I am contractually obliged to meet – and I also have other responsi-*ball*-ities (do you see what I did there?), so I am having to do some serious 'ball management'.

Thankfully, I share the glass ball that is 'The Kids' with Jimmy, so I've been able to pass that one over to him exclusively for a few days while I have been writing. Other balls – the podcast I usually record on Tuesday, my doctor's appointment, an appointment at the fracture clinic with my mum – I was able to delegate or temporarily put down. Some balls – the plastic ones – I didn't even worry about dropping. There were coffees I couldn't make, gym classes I had to cancel, and other stuff that I didn't even allow myself to worry about. Those balls are bouncing around somewhere and, when this book is done, I will have the bandwidth to be able to pick them up, unharmed, and carry on where I left off.

Almost all of the plastic balls (which, incidentally, were the ones that I held on to the tightest, and that often felt the heaviest) were actually really easy to put down temporarily when I needed to. So, sure, my house might look like a crack den, but I'm not on the verge of a total meltdown. I might not always be as polite as I could be, but I can always say sorry when I drop that ball. I might not eat as well as I want to for a few days, but that's okay. And if all that means that my brain is a little lighter to carry around with me, then that's a win.

Let me show you my balls. . .

Glass Balls
- Paying your bills
- Looking after your health and wellbeing
- Being kind to the people you love and who love you
- Taking accountability when you fuck up
- Making sure you are there for your kids
- Being a thoughtful and kind partner
- Practising an attitude of gratitude
- Getting enough sleep

Plastic Balls
- Any and all housework
- Meeting friends for social events
- Hair and make-up
- Worrying about your weight
- Getting dressed up
- Cooking meals from scratch
- Kids' birthday parties
- Baking vs buying birthday cakes
- Ironing
- Being at every school/sports event
- Answering every WhatsApp/email/phone call
- Deadlines
- Pleasing everyone
- Dressing your kids in stylish outfits
- Being on time every time
- Being polite and well-behaved
- Getting 10,000 steps in
- Not eating carbs
- Not eating sugar
- Any kind of restrictive eating

And then we have my favourite type of balls, which are actually not balls at all. Despite that, so many of us increase our mental loads by adding these 'Not Balls' into the mix:

Not Balls At All
- Fixing other people's problems
- Getting involved in other people's business
- Talking about other people when they're not in the room
- Worrying about what other people think

HANDLING YOUR BALLS

These are my balls, and while some of them may look like your balls too, they won't all be the same. I highly recommend looking closely at your balls and making sure you're handling them in the most efficient way.

Okay, that's enough about balls now.

18

The Self-Care Ball

'Caring for myself is not self-indulgence. It's self-preservation and that is an act of political warfare.' – Audre Lorde

I know I said that I wasn't going to talk about balls anymore, but then I remembered that the self-care ball is one that requires some serious examination – so, forgive me for a little more 'ball-talk'.

Self-care is a term that I've loved and hated in equal measure at different points in my role as the mental load bearer. It's been bandied around on social media since the dawn of inspirational quote tiles and I suspect, at times, it's pissed us all off. For a while there, we all fell into the trap of believing that a shower constituted self-care when, really, it's a basic human right. I think we're also guilty of thinking that a night out with the girls is self-care. I'm not saying getting mashed up with your mates isn't fun and even necessary, but if you go out with the girls like I used to go out with the girls, then there wasn't much 'care' involved in that.

It's taken me forty-three years, a couple of mental burnouts, thousands of hours of therapy, some hypnosis and three years of sobriety to realise that the odd night away in a hotel just doesn't cut it when it comes to self-care. Sure, it's fun, like a night out with your girlfriends, but you're not getting much recovery done because true self-care has to be sustained. I've realised that I can't just shoehorn the odd yoga or gym session in, the odd night away or early bedtime, and check the 'self-care' box on my to-do list. It doesn't work like that because, if it's another thing you have to organise, manage or stress over fitting in, then it's not doing you much good.

I think I've come to understand that truly effective self-care, for me at least, isn't about doing all the fun stuff I want to do. Self-care isn't running yourself into the ground and then taking a week to lie in the sun with your best friend. It's not martyring yourself and then demanding that everyone leave the house so that you can just have some time to yourself. It's not doing everything for everyone all week so that, come Saturday night, you can go to your best mate's house and get silly on Chardonnay. I promise you, I have tried all of these things and I still ended up burning out.

However, *I think* I've figured it out. Self-care for me is not about riding the rollercoaster of the highs and lows. I don't want to lose my shit at home so that I can go and lose my mind in a club in Soho. I don't want to burn the candle at both ends anymore. I've tried it and it's exhausting. I've spent too many years living in the extremes. As an addict in recovery, it won't surprise you to know that I'm not great at moderating but, when it comes to self-care, moderation is the secret sauce.

I suppose what I've come to understand is that my self-care

is closely tied to my own feelings of self-love and self-respect. It's also really a code word for being a fucking grown-up, because essentially it's been about learning when to say no and when to get up and do the things I don't really feel like doing because self-care doesn't always look like I want it to look. Do I wish that diving headfirst into a tub of Ben & Jerry's Half Baked ice cream, while sitting, un-showered, in my jammies, watching shit TV, is the self-care I need? Of course I do. But it isn't. It isn't what will keep my head calm and balanced. Instead, I have had to accept that self-care often starts from a much more mundane place. I've had to learn to schedule things properly so that I don't get overwhelmed, to get out of my own way and make sure I communicate my wants and needs effectively, and that to ask for help when doing so will ease the pressure. It's become about taking half an hour every day to be by myself, to put everything down and just check in with my body and my brain and figure out where any pain points are and why, and then do something about it.

I spent a long time being really mad that the people around me didn't just *know* that I needed help or space or time or a tub of Ben & Jerry's. Why weren't they helping? Couldn't they see how much I was struggling? No. They couldn't see, because while my internal monologue was freaking out, externally, I was absolutely fine. Even though my performance of being 'absolutely fine' was Oscar-worthy, I was furious that Jimmy seemed oblivious to the fact that I was on the Stress Superhighway heading for Burnout Boulevard. For some reason, I'd come to believe that it was someone else's responsibility to make space for my self-care. I don't know why I expected him to take me gently by the shoulder and suggest

I take some time out, but I do remember being offended when he never thought to book me a solo spa day, or surprise me with a romantic weekend away. It sounds terribly entitled – and it was – but I think, going back to what I was talking about in the Rom-Con chapter, in some warped way I'd decided that these big gestures were proof that he loved me when, in reality, the only thing it proved is that I was really shit at communicating my wants and needs.

As a teacher, I was always encouraged to use a real-world example to help explain an idea or a concept. So, in homage to that time of my life, here's what self-care looks like to me today.

Scheduling as self-care

First, let's talk about scheduling. Jimmy and I are both self-employed, so we don't have the luxury of being able to rely on a set routine. We don't wake up every morning and know that we're both going to shower, get dressed, get the kids ready and get out of the house. Some mornings we might have early work commitments, or some nights we might have to work late. Often we're both in the house during the day but a lot of the time we're out and about. There is no 9–5 for us. While this can be a wonderful way to live, it also leaves a lot of room for scheduling clusterfucks.

So, we do what most people do – we share a digital diary. Easy, right? We make sure that anything the other one absolutely *needs* to know about is in bright red and is sent via email as well. So far, so normal. In addition, though, we also have a daily Morning Meeting (sexy, I know) and a Sunday Huddle after the kids have gone to bed.

The Sunday Huddle is the main planning meeting. We look over our diaries and make sure they've got the same things in them for the week ahead. We talk through each day and make sure we've got drop-offs and pick-ups covered. We make sure we know who's playing taxi driver for extra-curricular activities and who's responsible for dinner each day. We talk about who's got what deadlines, where the pressure points are and figure out how to support each other with those.

But we also use this time to plan our own 'self-care' stuff. I'll make sure I've got any social stuff locked in: my regular gym sessions, recovery work and dog walks are protected time, and he'll do the same with his running and the social stuff he wants to do.

It sounds very 'rom-con', I know, but it's really not. It can get pretty heated, especially if we've both overbooked, or if we both have a really important work thing that clashes and we can't get childcare or (as is the case as I write this in the run-up to Christmas) the season just demands an unreasonable amount of social commitments from us. Rather than fight to the death over whose stuff is more important, we tend to resort to rock paper scissors these days. We have a pact that rock paper scissors is sacrosanct – the result unchallengeable. It's just easier that way.

The Sunday Huddle is also a great way of recognising when your scheduling is unrealistic. There's something about saying it out loud to someone that guarantees you see it for what it really is. I can't tell you the amount of times I've stopped midway through a Sunday Huddle and said something along the lines of, 'What the fuck was I thinking?!', only to resolve to cancel a load of shit STAT.

The Morning Meetings are a brief catch-up on what the day ahead looks like. We usually do it quickly over a cup of coffee (me) and tea (Jimmy). It will go something like this:

Me: So, I'm doing drop-off, you're doing pick-up, and Jo's going to take them to kickboxing? You've got dinner covered, right?

Jimmy: Yep – all good. I'm out all day but will be back around 5pm. What time do you want dinner?

Me: I won't be back until 6.30ish.

Jimmy: Cool.

Me: Don't forget to take that parcel to the post office and I'll sort the parking ticket today too.

Jimmy: Got it. Keep in touch.

Me: Yep.

And that's it. I don't think there's anything special about that, but there is something special about naming it the Morning Meeting. There's something magical about setting an intention for the conversation, something that makes us both mentally sit up and take responsibility for the myriad of shit that we have to be responsible for.

I've also learned that I don't have to say yes to every invitation and, even more importantly, I've learned that I can pull out of something if it becomes clear it's unmanageable. What I'm *not* going to do, though, is lie about it. I'm also not going to underestimate the negative consequences it might have on someone else. So, if, for example, I realise I just can't make it to something I've RSVP'd yes to, I'll let them know as soon as I can and I'll be honest. I won't make up sick kids, or scheduling conflicts. Instead I'll just say something along the lines of, 'I'm so sorry, I'm going to have to pull out tonight. I've realised – too late – that I've taken on too much this week. It's entirely my fault and I'm working on being better at this. Please let me know what I can do to make it up to you.' Sure, some people will still get upset, and justifiably so, but I'd rather have to apologise and make it up to them than run myself into an early grave.

Communication as self-care
I've learned over the years that things go tits up between Jimmy and I when I forget that *telepathy is not a reliable form of communication*. It turns out, I have spent my whole life being deathly afraid of being honest about how I was really feeling – mostly because I had no idea. I used to think anger was an emotion. Now I know it's actually just a shield. When I'm angry, I'm subconsciously working really hard to not feel what I'm actually feeling and I'm working even harder to never have to *admit* how I'm really feeling. Because to do that would be to show vulnerability. It would be letting someone into my deepest, darkest insecurities – and why the fuck would I want to do that?

When I'm angry and shouting, chances are I'm either feeling fear or pain. I'm either scared that the situation I find myself in is one that's going to prove I'm unlovable or unlike-able or not good enough, or I'm hurt and don't want to admit it because that means that whoever I'm angry at has the potential to reach into the soft and squishy parts of me and cause me pain. Both of those things terrify the shit out of me. Truly. The thought of either of those things being true brings the same ice-cold fear to my heart that waking up with a tarantula on my face would. And yet, ironically, those things happen quite a lot, because I'm human and I share my world with other humans. So, I've had to learn that rather than get angry and try to pretend those uncomfortable feelings away, I have to put my shield down and start communicating honestly.

Before I'd managed to figure all of that out, I'd get angrier and angrier as I wondered why he didn't just know I was struggling. It didn't end well and, I'm sure you already know this, but having an emotional vomit all over the people you love is not very 'self-carey'. What *is* self-carey, however, is figuring out how I'm really feeling, where that feeling came from, and how best to communicate that.

Once, I was driving the kids home from school and feeling tired, overworked and underappreciated. The kids saw the opportunity and played it well. 'Can we have McDonald's, Mum? You look like you could use a break from cooking. This way you can put your feet up when you get home.' Genius little ratbags. And so a McDonald's it was – I'd never felt more grateful for those glorious golden arches.

When we got home, the kids tucked into their food and five minutes later Jimmy came home.

'Oh, McDonald's for dinner! Mmm, what did you do to deserve that?'

'Nothing,' they replied. 'Mum just couldn't be bothered to cook dinner.'

Well, reader, I am sure you will not be surprised to learn that I went apeshit. Or maybe you will be surprised. I don't know. What I do know is that I was furious. Like, steam-coming-out-of-my-ears-and-arse furious. I felt like the kids had got what they wanted and then casually thrown me under the bus, even though, if I was really honest, I really couldn't be bothered to cook dinner and that was exactly why they were having McDonald's. On an *intellectual* level, I knew there was absolutely nothing wrong with that. On a lizard-brain, subconscious level, however, I was enraged. I felt attacked, criticised, shamed and isolated. I felt like they were a little team and I was the lazy, good-for-nothing, worse-than-average mum who couldn't even be arsed to pop a few frozen fish fingers in the oven and boil a few peas.

A therapy session later, it became clear that the lizard brain had won because the conversation, as brief as it was, had poked the bear of that very painful memory from the first few weeks of having my eldest daughter, Billie. It had ignited the very same feelings I'd felt when the health visitor had told me I'd damaged my baby by giving her formula. So, when I sniffed out an implicit criticism of how I was feeding my kids that day with the McDonald's, my poor, traumatised, deathly afraid subconscious went into free fall.

Just the hint of a suggestion that I might not be doing the absolute best for my children was enough to make me come out fighting, all guns blazing, when what I was really feeling was deep, unanaesthetised, searing emotional pain that I didn't even really know still existed there. Anyone else may have been able to laugh it off, not take it too seriously, but not me. I couldn't do it because there was a trauma there, like a jellyfish, and I was blissfully unaware of the way its tentacles had spread silently throughout the chambers of my brain and soul, ready to activate the sting of pain and shame whenever it got the chance.

To this day, I have to be hypervigilant of the residual pain that comment made by the health visitor caused me. I'm not over it. I'm not sure I ever will be – so deep was the wound. But, I am more aware of it than I've ever been and I keep that awareness close at all times to make sure that pain doesn't come out sideways, all over an unsuspecting person. And that's on me. That trauma wasn't my fault but it is my responsibility to learn how to communicate it without doing more damage. It's not easy and I don't always get it right, but at least I know I can fix my mistakes because now I know what caused them.

The point of this is to explain how some of the pressure I was feeling was actually not about the mental load itself. Some of it was stuff I was consciously or subconsciously bringing to the interactions I was having. As I scrolled through Instagram the other day, I heard something that resonated deeply. I wish I could remember who said it, but here it is anyway: 'If the reaction is above a 5, then it's about something else.'

Being by myself
Taking half an hour, every day, to be by yourself may not seem as fun or as 'caring' as taking a weekend away, but I promise you, it's the best way to maintain the balance. You can always take half an hour. There's always half an hour that can be mined from somewhere and I know that to be true because I used to believe it wasn't as easy as that.

The fact is, I didn't want to take half an hour. I wanted to take the day, or three hours, and half an hour didn't feel like enough, but this isn't half an hour to get a load of shit done. The point of this half an hour is that you don't do anything, and by anything I mean even scrolling through your phone. I use that half an hour to literally walk my brain up and down my body and check what's going on. It's wild to me that I only started doing this recently. I spent decades literally not listening to my body and it was no wonder my body ended up saying 'Fuck you' and shutting down.

I look for physical pain (always my bloody left Achilles, sometimes my lower back, my tummy if I've eaten badly or I'm on my period, occasionally my head). I look for feelings of anxiety. Sometimes they hide in my head, my throat or my tummy. The throat ones are the worst. Sometimes they make me feel like I can't breathe. I rifle through my mental filing cabinets and try to isolate thoughts that I'm struggling with, things that make me feel uncomfortable. Towards the end, I try to decide how many of those things that make me feel uncomfortable or in pain I have control over and how many I need to let go of. It can be as simple as taking paracetamol for a headache. But, it can also be about girding my loins to call someone and apologise if I've realised I need to take responsibility for something. If I can't do anything about the stuff that's bothering me, I say a little prayer and move on: *Grant me the serenity to accept the things I cannot change, courage to change the things I can and wisdom to know the difference.*

Finally, if I can get into good habits when it comes to scheduling, communication and small pockets of alone time to check in with my brain and body, I know I am really looking after myself. I know that, because I have more patience, I'm kinder to myself and others, I'm more effective as a business owner, a mother, a wife, a friend. Self-care isn't something I wait for someone to grant me anymore. It's something I've learned to ask for, prioritise and maintain, in the same way I maintain good oral health. Self-care is emotional flossing.

19

If Weaponised Incompetence Were a Person, it Would Be a Kid

'Helping out at home raises self-esteem: when parents insist that kids do their chores, they are letting them know that they are not just loved; they are needed.' – Wendy Hughes

If you're reading this book and you don't have kids, then good for you. Seriously, I salute you. I love my kids and I wouldn't ever want to be without them, but I can't promise you that if I'd had a 'try before you buy' option, I would have committed after the free trial was up. It's just that, in the beginning especially, the work/reward balance is really skewed, and it takes years to get it back on track. I'm eleven years in and boy do I love those tiny terrorists, and while it's easier in a lot of ways because they can wipe their own butts and put their own shoes on, it's harder in others. As I mentioned earlier – hormones are a bitch.

It's not their fault. They're just doing what miniature humans with undeveloped prefrontal cortexes do, which is march through the world like it's theirs, giving off the air of a particularly despicable Roman emperor. As parents, we wake up anxious about what lies in the day ahead. Will it be a metaphorical thumbs-up day or a thumbs-down day from our progeny?

Thumbs-up days are great – minimal tantrums, they ate what they were given (regardless of what colour plate it was delivered on) and went to bed without a battle. Thumbs-down days are not so great. They're the days where nothing you do is right. They're the days when the kids want to wear their wellies on the wrong feet, just because. They're the days when you've cut the sandwiches wrong, you left the snacks behind, nap time went down the drain, which was probably blocked, and it all ended in tears.

They're kids! What can we expect? Well, controversially, I'm starting to realise we can expect a lot more from them than we do . . . or at least that's been true in my experience. Let's be honest, when it comes to the mental load, kids are the real villains of the story. Of course we love them and of course we want to do everything and anything to make sure they are safe and happy, it's just that, on top of everything else, it can feel like an impossible task.

To keep a small human alive – let's say one aged four or under – you have to pretty much be with them all the time. I think that bears repeating – if you have children aged four and under, you have to be with them *all the time*. Every goddamn mother-loving, air-breathing second of the day and night, they cannot be left alone. Not even, really, in another room while you take a shit, because you just know that if you dared to do that, you would come out to discover they'd drawn all over the walls, or set the cat on fire. It's a relentless, often thankless task that until we're in it ourselves we can never fully comprehend.

And, it's not as if, during this period of constant child-keeping, you get to absent yourself from the multitude of other worldly responsibilities. Most of us still have to work, we all have to do laundry, clean and cook, exercise, sleep and make time for other humans in our lives – including ones our own age. So, when you think about it like that, it's a miracle women with small children are even able to construct a full sentence.

I think what happens is, during this period, we get so used to doing everything for them that we forget that it wasn't *that* long ago they were expected to clamber up chimneys to earn their keep. I'm not suggesting we bring back child labour, but I do think as they get a bit older there are things we can start to hand over to them. Even if we are aware that they could help out more, suggesting it is often met with the kind of resistance that only a deeply irritated five-year-old can dish out, so it's understandable that we back down fairly quickly. You see, I've come to the conclusion that kids, much like men, have figured out how to weaponise their incompetence. In a man, that skill is sickening and deeply unattractive, but in a five-year-old, I can't help but be a little impressed by it. They are completely unable to tie a shoelace, but they appear to have mastered emotional manipulation fluently. Go figure.

Yes, it's ironic that the smallest people in the house tend to come with the longest list of stuff you need to do for them but – unpopular opinion incoming – I think we're guilty of mollycoddling the little crotch goblins. I know this because I've done it for years and here's why: it's easier to just bloody do it myself. It's that simple. When it comes to kids, it's all about short-term pain for long-term gain.

Please know that, as I write this, I am itchy with hypocrisy because I am the first to hop, skip and jump over to the path of least resistance. I'm also not beyond getting really resentful about it and entirely forgetting that I created my own monsters. But the benefit of hindsight has made it abundantly clear to me that kids are capable of far more than we expect of them.

One of my very best friends lives in Denver, Colorado, and she is the absolute boss when it comes to expecting her kids to do things for themselves. I mention her because we only see them intermittently, but every time we do hang out, I always leave having picked up a million excellent habits that I implement immediately.

The first of these habits I learned when my eldest was about three. We were visiting my friend in Colorado and we'd all had dinner together. When we'd finished eating, my friend Reagan looked at her eldest, who was four, and said, 'Please take care of your responsibilities.' The kid got up, without a sigh, a tut or a curl of the lip, picked up his plate and his knife and fork, and took it to the sink. He then came, sat back down, and asked if he could leave the table.

Jimmy and I looked at each other agog. What was this witchery? Why did our kids not take their own plates to the sink? Were we terrible parents? Honestly, and I can say this with my hand on my heart, it had never occurred to me to ask them. In a lot of ways, it's not ideal, right? Everyone has to get up to take one plate to the sink – it feels inefficient – but I quickly realised this whole thing wasn't about the convenience of it all. It was about the principle of it all. The kids were expected to do the things they could do.

We implemented this immediately and the results were

spectacular. It helped that they'd seen their friend do it and the praise he'd received for being a 'really good boy' hadn't gone unnoticed either. Now that my girls are eight and eleven, they are expected to clear the table completely after every meal, including wiping it down. It's just done – we don't even have to ask. I'm not saying this to show off, and I'm not suggesting that getting your kids to clear their plates away is going to reduce the weight of your mental load in any way, but in a very tiny, very almost-unnoticeable way, it starts to show the kids that there are a lot of things that go on in the house that don't just happen. It's the first death knoll to the myth of the cleaning fairies.

Reagan also introduced me to the concept of Chores vs. Responsibilities. We wanted to give the kids pocket money, but we wanted to use it as an opportunity to help them understand the idea of earning money and managing it. Reagan explained that they had a list of chores and a list of responsibilities. Responsibilities were the things that they *didn't* get cash for because these were about looking after their own shit; responsibilities are the things that all functioning humans are expected to be able to do. For example, responsibilities may include making your bed, keeping your own room tidy, putting your own clean laundry away, bringing your own dirty laundry down, tidying up after yourself in communal areas.

Chores, on the other hand, are things that are about helping the family out as a whole and *this* is where it starts to get interesting regarding the mental load. Chores are things that have to be done, that are usually done by me and often aren't even noticed by anyone else I live with (or at least not acknowledged). The cool thing about chores is that there are loads of chores that even small kids can do and, because they are *actually* helpful, then earning pocket money for these things seems valid. I've put together a list of chores below that our kids often take responsibility for.

Chores
- Refilling loo rolls in the bathrooms
- Bringing everyone's dirty laundry down
- Stripping beds
- Bringing dirty towels down and replacing them with clean ones
- Picking up dog poo in the garden
- Feeding and watering the dog (looking after pets)
- Washing/cleaning pets
- Watering the plants
- Cleaning out the crap in the car
- Wiping down the skirting boards
- Putting their sibling's laundry away
- Emptying all the bins
- Loading/unloading the dishwasher
- Sweeping and tidying the front porch
- Setting the table
- Dusting
- Organising the books/toys in their rooms
- Sorting laundry (whites/coloureds/darks)
- Dog walking (age/area dependent)
- Vacuuming
- Mopping
- Writing thank-you cards
- Clearing out for the charity shop

- Help put the shopping away
- Shine up knives and forks by hand
- Organising a drawer of doom

This isn't an exhaustive list, and some of these take a little training, but there's nothing on this list that kids can't do.★

Weekends used to be such a pain point for me. Everyone else I live with appeared to approach them as if they were looking down the barrel of two full days off. They'd kick their shoes off, throw their uniform/running gear on the floor and systematically move from room to room, leaving a trail of domestic destruction in their wake while I frantically tried to clean every room, change every bed, dust every surface, wash all the clothes and complete the myriad of other tasks that ran through my brain.

When my husband gently pointed out one weekend that I tended to be really angry every Saturday and Sunday, two things occurred to me:

1. I'd been relying on telepathy as a reliable form of communication.
2. I needed to make it clear what was happening behind the scenes.

So, I started the TWATT List (Team Work All The Time List). On a Saturday morning I write a list of all the things that need doing around the house and I put my initials next to the ones that I'm going to do. Then I pop the list on the

★ Of course, not *all* kids can do *all* of these things. A lot of this is age dependent, but I've found it really helpful to keep this list in mind as my kids grow, learn and become more independent.

kitchen table, with a pen, and everyone else puts their initials next to the jobs that they're going to do. It's worked really well and when someone doesn't do their job, it's easy to call out the culprit. I don't think Billie will ever forget the time she forgot to restock the bathrooms with loo roll. Jimmy was caught short on his morning poo, in the house alone, and had to do a danger-run to the laundry room to collect some bog roll. It wasn't a pretty sight.

I know that, for some of you, the thought of writing a list makes you bristle with indignation. *But*, I hear you holler in knackered and frustrated tones, *isn't 'write the list' just another thing that I have to add to my to-do list?* I don't know – maybe. I know that I always wrote a list anyway, whether I was doing it all myself or not. But I also think that we need to accept our partner and our kids the way they are and not the way we want them to be. None of them have been trained in the same way that we as women have – whether implicitly or not – and so, like it or not, it may be that we have to spend some time showing them the way of the mental load. It may well be the responsibility of our generation to train our partners and our children in the secret ways of the mental load. I didn't say it was fair; but it might be necessary.

As I said, short-term pain for long-term gain.

I get your frustration, though. I really do. It is frustrating because it feels like our generation is responsible for fixing the mistakes of the generations that have gone before us. It feels like we're clearing up someone else's mess (physically and metaphorically). But I think that's part of our contribution to the evolution of society as millennial women. We're the cycle-breakers, the load-sharers, the way-finders. It's a job we didn't ask for, sure, but it's a job that will have endlessly positive repercussions for all our sons and daughters and our grandsons and granddaughters.

So writing a list, spelling out the obvious, getting sick of the sound of your own voice – these things may just be the price we pay as the architects of a seismic, social shift, and when you think about it like that, we're basically Avenger-style superheroes.

20

Doing it for the 'Gram

'Even though you can logically understand that it's curated, that doesn't change the fact that continuous scrolling through idealized lives can breed feelings of inadequacy and discontent, fuelling a cycle of comparison and envy.' – Solane Bramhill, *The Comparison Trap: Social Media and Mental Health envy.* [4]

Ahhh, social media. Is there any topic on earth that doesn't require us to scrutinise the role that social media plays in it? I'm not sure there is anymore. It's so invasive within our everyday existence that it seems to affect everything we think, feel and do. Therefore, there's no way, as a content creator myself, I can get away without discussing the role of social media within the context of the mental load.

Let me begin by saying that I don't think the effect of social media in relation to the mental load has been all bad. There's no doubt that social media has been instrumental in creating a space for the conversation about the mental load to take place. It has facilitated a connection among all types of women, from all over the world, every community and generation together to share in a discussion that we previously haven't been able to have. In many ways, it's unionised us. It's empowered us to make changes because social media has shown that this isn't an individual problem but a social issue which all women, to a greater or lesser extent, are affected by – and that, I truly believe, is a good thing. But there are, of course, some downsides.

All the research suggests that women use social media more than men, although the gap is lessening,[5] which would also suggest that the negative effects of social media are likely affecting women more than men. From a personal point of view, I have spent a considerable amount of time on social media for the last ten years and there's no doubt it's affected my mental health significantly. That doesn't mean to say that I'm struggling, but it has been necessary to adjust the ways I consume social media and manage the platforms I spend time on to effectively counter its impact.

Teddy Roosevelt said that comparison is the thief of joy and, while I'm not one for an inspirational quote, on this subject he was spot on. When you think about it, at the most basic level, social media's *raison d'être* is to serve up fodder for us to assess ourselves against. I think women are, in general, more deeply affected by the pressure of comparison than men are. It's not a scientific fact, but my female intuition tells me this is so and there's nothing more damaging, in my opinion, to the modern woman than the aspirational content that exists online.

Sure, we've seen this dynamic before, online and offline, when it comes to bodies and beauty, but, thanks to social media, we are now able to compare bed frames, front porches,

Christmas trees, Sunday roasts, pumpkin-carving abilities, cleaning skills, utility rooms, and even our relationships. As we scroll mindlessly through social media, we are often unaware of the way in which each picture can make us feel like failures. If you spend ten minutes scrolling, that's a hundred mini-failures we are likely to have experienced. That's got to be beating the shit out of our mental health on a significant level hour after hour, day after day.

I have a lovely house, but I hate my house. I have a big house, but it's not quite big enough. My kettle is fine, but it could be better. My utility room does the job, but it's not aesthetically pleasing. My kids are great, but their clothes always have a stain on them – why?? I don't have the time to lay a beautiful table every evening, or to paint my living room every six months. I can't put furniture and accessories together in the way I wish I could, and this feeling of general malaise doesn't come from nowhere, does it? When these feelings of inadequacy are laid over the generalised anxiety that stems from the mental load, it can feel like an impossibly overwhelming task to know how to begin tackling it all, let alone achieving it all.

Everything that every woman has ever feared, social media appears to prove to be true. It shows us that there are women out there who can have it all and do it all. Time and time again, it confirms that there are women who have a beautiful, big house that is always tidy and clean, stylishly decorated and that they are capable of transforming it into a factory of magical memory-making every Halloween, Easter, Christmas and birthday. These women also tend to be thin, beautiful and as stylish as their shelfies – I said it at the beginning, pretty privilege is a thing and it's never more apparent than on social media. Their husbands are often gorgeous and adorably reluctant to be on social media. They're endlessly supportive and appear to look at their wives with such admiration that I sometimes wonder if they're drugged. These women cook a perfect meal every night, while also looking perfectly fuckable to their husbands and, simultaneously, perfectly nurturing to their children. Their cars are shiny, their garages organised. They don't have cupboards of doom, or shit shoe racks bursting at the seams in their hallways.

These women have the money and the childcare to take luxurious weekends away with their husbands at Soho Farmhouse, where they almost certainly shag like rabbits – no cystitis for them, of course! They are the type of people who always come home from holiday to a pristine house and unpack the minute they get home. They label mason jars and fill them with unprocessed foods and line them up perfectly in sleek pantries. There are never coffee stains on their kitchen cabinets or random socks lying around. They don't appear to be drowning in laundry and their kids don't seem to leave any of their plastic tat lying around for them to stand on or trip up over.

Meanwhile, the muggles like you and me can't even find a minute to blow-dry our hair or remember to book a dentist appointment for the kids. Our instinct isn't to see these paragons of domestic perfection as the exception to the rule. No, our instinct is to see their perfection as a baseline, and our reality, and therefore ourselves, as woefully under-achieving examples of womanhood. Why is it, we ask ourselves, that in their lives, the mental load isn't just invisible, but appears non-existent? Why can't I do what they do when they make it look so easy? What is wrong with me that means I find it all so difficult? Are their lives easy because they're perfect, or are their lives perfect because they find it easy? Well, neither of those things are true because, of course, it's all total and utter bollocks.

Intellectually, there isn't a woman in the world who doesn't know that the perfection we see on social media is bollocks, but it affects us nonetheless. And, when I say 'affects us', what I mean is it pours hot lava on the mental load in our brains so that we, quite literally, go into meltdown. In preparation for writing this chapter, I dedicated an hour to consciously scrolling through social media and really taking the time and effort to consider how each and every post *really* made me feel. Firstly, I realised it was almost an impossible task. Social media is designed to be consumed unconsciously, so stopping myself slipping into a zombie-like stupor was a gargantuan exercise. It was also incredibly difficult to 'right-size' what I was seeing. I had to make a conscious effort to critically assess everything and remind myself what was real and what wasn't. I put my phone down after that hour, hating everything about my house, feeling an impulse to spend a load of money on paint and furniture to make it better and, to top it off, I'd lost an hour to scrolling when I should have been preparing dinner. It was a double sucker-punch.

Secondly, I didn't really like what I felt. I felt really uncom-fortable with the feelings of jealousy that I experienced. It didn't make me think nice thoughts about people, or make me want to act in a way that was supportive, kind and forgiving. I didn't feel happy for many people. A couple of times, I had to go back and force myself to like a post and comment on it kindly and supportively because I *knew* it was the right thing to do, but for some reason, I didn't *feel* like I wanted to. Unless I am constantly alert to the time I spend on social media, what kind of content I consume, and how I process the content I see, it can quite quickly and easily make me feel itchy, twitchy and bitchy and behave like the worst possible version of myself. Add those feelings of inadequacy and jealousy to the weight of the pre-existing, in-your-real-life mental load, and it's not a healthy mix.

When we see those snippets of someone's life on social media – the 'highlight reel' as they like to say – it's easy to forget it's just a tiny, pixelated, square snapshot of a single second in their life. We can remind ourselves, after the fact, that their life probably isn't as perfect as it looks, and that they almost certainly still fight with their husband over the loo seat being left up, and occasionally they must lock themselves in the bathroom and have a good cry too, but by then, the damage to our psyche has been done. Those feelings of failure, jealousy, sadness and inadequacy have already been felt. They can be mitigated, but they can't be *un*felt, and when we're doing that repeatedly, for hours and hours a day, it's no wonder we feel like shit.

Social media has, arguably, done more to increase the pressure of the mental load than any patriarchal society could do, and I have to acknowledge my part in that. You could inject me with truth serum and I would die telling you that I am authentic and honest and my true self on there. I would bet both my ovaries on the fact that I show the snotty, ugly, messy, dirty reality of my life on social media, but that's only half the story. No matter how hard I try to not make someone feel bad about themselves, my content will inevitably do just that. It's all relative. My messy house is someone else's palace. My make-up-free, knackered face is someone else's unattainable beauty standard. My annoying husband is someone else's perfect man (okay, that might be a bit of a stretch!). The point is, no matter how careful you are with the content you make, or the content you consume, it's potentially harmful to someone else's mental health and can make their mental load feel heavier.

I have so much to be thankful to social media for. It's enabled me to make a living in a way I never thought I'd be able to; it's given me a community, a sense of self and a set of values that I wouldn't have been able to define as clearly if it weren't for the harsh lens of social media. It's provided me with an opportunity to do for a living what I always wanted to do but never thought would be possible – to write books, like the one you're reading now. I'd be lying if I didn't admit that it saddens me to think how content, how less stressed, or less hard on myself I would be if social media wasn't the soundtrack to my life. I make an effort to be grateful for all the things I have in my life, but maybe, if I didn't deep-dive into my Instagram feed every day, the effort to be grateful wouldn't need to be so great? I don't know and I'll never know because – and this is wild – we are the very last generation on earth to know what life was like before social media.

What I do know is that, however perfect a life appears to be on social media, there isn't a woman in the world who's exempt from the pressures of the mental load and from what it's like to exist in a world that wasn't designed for them. Even if their cage is gilded and filled with expensive furniture, that mental load still exists somewhere behind the scenes and with it the constant mental strain that they choose *not* to show on Instagram. And maybe, in the end, showing the perfect parts of their life is the way they cope with managing the imperfect parts.

Social media is a genie we cannot put back in the bottle and, as I like to remind myself daily, I have to accept the world the way it is and not be angry because it's not the way I want it to be. I can't expect people to make content that doesn't upset or trigger me. People can create whatever content they want and, even if it has a negative impact on me, it might do the opposite for someone else. Social media is certainly problematic, but it's not necessarily the problem. The problem is what I allow into my consciousness and what happens when I forget to be responsible for the content I see and interact with.

The only thing *I* can do is adjust how *I* move through the social media world. While digesting less social media may not always be possible for an instawanker like me, it is necessary for me to be much more conscious about what I digest and when I digest it. If the content I consume on social media has a negative effect on my mental health, and/or makes the pressure of my real-life mental load harder to bear, then it is *my responsibility* to address that balance.

Like it or not, I know those big tech companies are not going to rescue me from the negative impacts of social media. Only I can do that. I have had to become hyperconscious of the impact it has on me when I slip into bad habits like doomscrolling, scrolling late at night or first thing in the morning. Not only does it suck my time away, therefore causing me to be stressed about the mental load stuff I haven't managed to get done, but any get-up-and-go has got-up-and-gone after a lengthy doomscroll. I cannot allow myself to compare my unedited life to the highlights reels of others because if we're always assessing our own capacity to manage the mental load through the lens of those we see managing their's seemingly effortlessly on social media, we are always going to feel defeated.

21

The Men-tal Load

'Good men and women do exist but sometimes you have to stop focusing on what's wrong with them and start looking for what's right. They might not be perfect, but nor are you. Stop keeping your expectations so high; especially when you don't meet those expectations yourself.' – Vex King

How many times have you considered that men might be carrying their own mental load? Before the day we walked into couples' therapy, I can tell you how many times I considered the idea that Jimmy may also be carrying his own mental load: zero, *nada*, not once. I was so wrapped up in my own self-pity-party regarding all the things he never made an effort to see or understand, that it literally never occurred to me that he could be struggling under the weight of another set of expectations. When it comes down to it, that's where the mental load comes from: expectations. Expectations that society has constructed, that our parents modelled, that social media boosted around the world, and that books, films and songs promote with zero disclaimers.

All my romantic relationships with men have been, in some way, warped by the gender expectations I felt the weight of. Until I met Jimmy, being myself in a relationship with a man felt impossible when I also had to be the woman/girlfriend that I felt society expected me to be.

My very first love was a tall boy who was absolutely gorgeous by anyone's standards. He played basketball and was a competitive sprinter, his parents owned a pub and he grew up in the Yorkshire Dales among Young Farmers who played rugby – but he'd spend his afternoons writing poetry and reading classics. We were together for about four or five years and, because the internet didn't yet exist, we sent each other letters declaring our undying love for each other every week from boarding school. I would read out the letters he sent to my girlfriends as we huddled in our dormitory and they would swoon over the romance of it all. When we broke up, I was heartbroken in the way you are the first time it happens. I'm not sure I've ever fully recovered from the internal fracture that losing that love caused. Do you ever recover fully from the loss of your first love?

The second love of my life was an artist. I was eighteen when we met and he was eight years older than me. He was witty, charming, totally lacking in self-consciousness, good-looking and socially magnetic. When he spoke to you he made you feel like you were the only person in the room. I was infatuated, but underneath his bravado, there was also vulnerability, pain and fear. I saw myself in him – a chameleon, a character, a shiny bright thing that would turn to dust if anyone ever really got beyond the performance. Somewhat inevitably – probably due to the age difference, my lack of confidence and his obvious commitment issues – he treated me terribly. He picked me up and put me down when it suited him and I let him. I entertained fantasies that I would be the one to change him and make him want to settle down, so I tried to be everything I thought he wanted me to be. In the end, I lost myself entirely and it took me a long time to begin to put the pieces of myself back together.

After him came the man I may well have married if I'd had my shit together. He was Australian, kind, charming, open, vulnerable, honest and able to communicate in a way I had never encountered before. I was too broken by the artist, though, to ever be in a position to let anyone get as close as this man wanted to. I pretended for a while and, at one point, thought I might pull it off, but the damage to my defences had been done and the rebuild was so complete and impenetrable that he never had a chance. I wish I'd treated him better.

Then there was the guy who was a port in the storm. I worked in a ski resort for a season and it didn't go well for me. I thought it would be the best four months of my life, but it was cliquey and I was bullied and I didn't cope very well. I attached myself to him – he was also kind of an outlier – I think mostly for protection than anything else. When the season came to an end, so too did the relationship. Or, at least, it did on my end. But, back in the UK, for months afterwards, he would keep turning up at the weirdest places telling me we were meant to be together. I see now that I used him and then abandoned him when I didn't need him anymore. I'm not proud of that, but sometimes we do questionable things to protect ourselves.

What followed was a period of fucking around and finding out. In reality, there was probably a lot more fucking around than finding out, but that's what your twenties are for, right? Throughout the whole process, I was trying out different versions of men and the masculinity they represented. When I met Jimmy, I think what intrigued me the most was the disconnect between what he was – a musician – and who he was – a deeply sensitive, emotional guy who had a metric fuck tonne of issues and wasn't afraid to talk about them. It was his quietness that was different. With all the other men I'd dated or fallen in love with, there was a constant unsettled feeling in my stomach. I'd be constantly questioning where they were, who they were with, whether I could trust them, whether they were going to call or text. It was exhausting. With Jimmy, though, there was a peace in our connection that left me feeling safe and secure. I knew he would call. I knew he really fucking liked me. I knew that he wanted to be with me. The absence of that emotional chaos can, I think, sometimes be mistaken for emotional boredom, but to this day I am so grateful that something inside me told me to trust the peace.

It took many heartbreaks for me to figure out that a good man wasn't one who was ridiculously good-looking or the life and soul of the party. It wasn't about being treated mean and kept keen. It wasn't about whether he was rich or successful or desired by all women. It was about being able to talk honestly with someone without pretending to be someone I wasn't. It was about an initial feeling that, for some unknowable reason, my heart was safe with this man.

When my dad met my husband for the first time, they did

not understand each other. Jimmy didn't 'banter' in the same way my family did. It's not that he wasn't funny, but he just didn't buy into beating each other up verbally and calling it a joke, which was basically how I thought every family interacted. He also wasn't a 'businessman'. He was a creative, a musician, who turned up on my parents' doorstep wearing skinny jeans, his hair covering his eyes and rolling a cigarette (yeah, he didn't exactly do himself any favours). Three weeks before I introduced him to my parents, my dad asked me if I thought Jimmy was 'the one'. I replied that, yes, I did think he was. My dad squeezed my hand and told me he was happy for me. When he opened the door and came face to face with my skinny-jean-wearing, floppy-haired, smoking, musician boyfriend, he turned around to me and said clearly, so that we could all hear, 'Really, darling? *This* is the one?'

They are very different men and they both grew up with very different versions of what 'being a man' looked like. For a couple of years, they prowled around each other, uncertain as to whether they had anything in common. There was no animosity. They were polite and chatted but the conversation was always more stilted than fluent. It worried me on a number of levels. I loved my dad deeply, and if he didn't 'get' Jimmy, then was I even with the right person? If Jimmy couldn't fit into my family, should I even bother trying to squeeze him in? Thankfully, there was something inside me that told me to persevere, that Jimmy was indeed 'the one' and that, in time, it would work itself out, and even if it didn't, maybe it was a good thing I wasn't marrying a version of my father?

What transpired was something I'm not sure even I could have predicted. Jimmy didn't bend to fit my dad's expectations of what his daughter's husband should look like. He didn't wear a mask or put on a front. Jimmy was unapologetically Jimmy and it wasn't always easy for him. There were, I'm sure, many times when Jimmy felt deeply uncomfortable in my family, especially around the men, but he was never anything but himself. He continued on his path of quietness, calmness and kindness and slowly but surely, my dad and the other men in my family started to bend, to relax, to shake off the cloak of masculinity and trust Jimmy, even if they didn't fully understand him.

Being with Jimmy showed me that there was a different version of masculinity that I had not previously seen. It wasn't necessarily better, but I began to realise that it was better for me. My house had been full of masculine energy – my dad was a huge presence in the household, a big character and someone who leaned into the traditional roles of men and women pretty seriously – and I had taken a lot of that masculine energy on, I think in part because it seemed clear to me that masculine energy was going to get me further than the feminine energy I saw around me. I'd often been labelled a 'tomboy' or a 'daredevil'. People used to say, 'She's got no fear, that one,' and the irony was, they had no idea how wrong they were, but the chance to reveal that fear was never on offer. With Jimmy, it was different. I could be honest about my fear, my insecurities, my deep-seated worries, and he didn't judge or tell me to pull myself together. He wasn't embarrassed and didn't make me feel ashamed and I loved him – I love him – for that.

Jimmy was also a crier. He did and still does love a big cry, and I'm ashamed to admit that, at first, I found his propensity for tears deeply unattractive. I had never seen a man cry. In all honesty, I hadn't seen that many grown women cry either. It just wasn't done in our family. We didn't let those big feelings out in any way, shape or form, so when my husband started blubbing, I would get itchy all over. I would retreat with feelings of disgust bubbling under the surface. I knew enough to know that my reaction was not okay – that the problem was me – but I didn't know how to stop those feelings from coming up. Rather than want to comfort him, I wanted to run away and, like I'd always been taught, tell him to pull himself together. To my shame, Jimmy could feel the repulsion in me and I hated myself for it, but I had no idea how to override it.

I can only imagine how that made him feel. There I was, holding on to my old-fashioned, unrealistic expectations of what it was to be a 'man', and here was Jimmy, failing miserably in my eyes. As much as I wanted him to be a modern man who helped with the cleaning and shared the mental load, I didn't want him to be *so* modern that he cried about stuff. I wanted him to be around and help with the kids, but I also wanted him to provide financially so that we could have the life I so desperately thought would make me happy. That's the truth and I'm not proud of it.

The more time I spent with Jimmy, the more I began to gravitate towards his version of what it was to be a man. The version of masculinity that was within my family became jarring, overbearing and sometimes uncomfortable to be around. It wasn't that they were horrible people – I love them all deeply – but I found myself breathing a sigh of relief when Jimmy and I would leave and return to our newly formed bubble. Jimmy's emotional side made me feel less awkward as I leaned into my own vulnerability. It wasn't that he was a man and crying about his feelings; it was, I realised, that he was crying *at all*. I learned to dig beneath my own anger and figure out what the real feelings were and, annoyingly, I also became a crier. Who'd have thunk it?

When I started dating as a young teenager, I was focused on what men gave me, how they treated me, how they made me feel. I made them my higher power. They were responsible, in my eyes, for making me happy. When I met Jimmy, something changed. I understood instinctively that I could be my own person in this partnership, that it was my responsibility and mine alone to make myself happy. Jimmy made room for me, as I was and not how he wanted me to be. Of course, we weren't perfect and we managed to fuck it up spectacularly (most of this book is dedicated to that fact!), but the foundations of respect for each other as individuals in our own right were there from the beginning. Jimmy was the first man I didn't lose myself to in some way. I don't know what it was about Jimmy that broke through the tough-girl facade. It's clear that I'd spent my whole romantic life looking for a different version of the men I'd grown up with. None of my previous boyfriends had been 'alpha' males. It's only with hindsight that I realise that they all had that sensitivity, that emotional vulnerability in common.

What has my dating history got to do with a discussion on the mental load? I guess it's about deep-diving into my personal perceptions of men, my own expectations of them and my part in the pain that was caused. It's about analysing my patterns of behaviour and my actions and expectations that brought me to certain conclusions about how I should act, how things should look and what a good partner is, part of which was me believing that my role as the perfect girlfriend was to be the nurturer, the woman willing to do anything for her man. I *wanted* to cook and clean for these men to prove to them that I was the best girl they'd ever meet. Of course, I was also hyper-aware that I needed to be sexy, witty, charming and successful as well, and let me tell you, that's exhausting even when you're in your twenties.

A woman's mental load is intense, there's no doubt about it, but I wonder if it's become so much a part of the modern zeitgeist simply because there has been no space for it to be aired previously. It's always been there, but we haven't always been able to talk about it without being shut down, eye-rolled or reminded how grateful we should be. We've spent centuries questioning our own thoughts and feelings and wondering how we ended up with the dodgy shrimp in the domestic stew, only to be repeatedly told that we've got nothing to complain about. After all, we've got men to protect us, right? No one ever considered the irony that, as well as being our protectors, men were also our predators. Such a dynamic has never made for a safe space to stand up for ourselves in the face of intense generational gaslighting.

In contrast, discussions around men and the expectations put on them have been batted around for millennia. There's a reason there's idiomatic language around the caveman as the 'hunter-gatherer' and not around the cavewoman. As a species, we have instinctively felt the need to identify men and masculinity and, in doing so, have ensured a steady stream of analysis around it – a space in which the many thoughts and feelings of men about men can be shared. We have, since time began, grappled with the expectations of men and what it means to be a man, and while that doesn't necessarily make it easier for men, I do think it helps that the discussion about the expectations placed on them has been out in the open and acknowledged. The concept of what it means to be a man and the pressures that come with it have been validated in a way that a woman's experience hasn't.

We only have to look to artistic endeavours to show the prominence of the discussion around the pressures placed upon men throughout history. Shakespeare couldn't get enough of it. Hamlet grapples with social expectations of male behaviour and his general distaste for women; Macbeth falls foul of that most male of attributes – ambition; and Henry V leans into the performative aspects of masculinity in a leadership role. *Death of a Salesman* by Arthur Miller is a devastating account of a man broken under the expectations of American masculinity, while *A Streetcar Named Desire* is a violent depiction of male aggression. None of these narratives end well for the men involved, which, in itself, is also problematic. It's actually pretty difficult to think of artistic depictions of masculinity where the men didn't fall foul of their negative attributes.

If, for a minute, we as women can put aside our rage and our resentment (all perfectly valid, by the way) and consider the male experience in the way we wish they would consider ours, we may start to feel a little more compassion for the men in our lives. While we were learning how to run a household as little girls, boys were learning that, in order to be a 'man', they must be strong, ready to fight, able to balance their primitive aggressive nature with charm, savvy and success. The men of our generation weren't always lucky enough to have the role of a 'good father and husband' modelled for them. Many of them saw what we saw – a woman at home, taking care of all things domestic, while the man went out to earn a living, came home whenever he wanted and often popped back out to the pub for a pint. If we accept the unfairness of our mental load as a hangover from outdated and old-fashioned ideas about family and femininity, then, surely, we also must accept that men are bearing the burden of the same thing?

There's an uncomfortable truth that I'm learning to get comfortable with. My relationship history shows that *I* brought the mental load with me into every relationship I've ever had. Being 'the perfect woman' always, with every man I've known, included presenting a homemaker version of myself alongside the horny wet-dream version. Unlike the boxes and bags I turned up with when I moved in with Jimmy, I snuck this baggage in under the cover of darkness. I decided, on some level, that being a good cook, keeping a clean house, managing the schedules and all the other stuff was my way of showing Jimmy that I loved him and, if I'm honest, I spent a lot of time in the early days of our relationship protecting that role and not letting him anywhere near it. Could it be that it was less his expectation that I would 'sort it', 'do it', 'organise it' and more my own expectations that that's what a good woman does?

When I think about our own experience, I know that by far the biggest pressure that Jimmy felt as a man in a cis-heteronormative society was that of being the breadwinner.

Before kids, it was about him being able to contribute equally to the economic partnership. At the beginning of our relationship, I had a proper job with a regular monthly salary. Jimmy, on the other hand, was a self-employed musician and felt a lot of pressure to ensure he earned enough money to cover his half. We both knew, on an unspoken level, that worst-case scenario, I could cover the bills, and I think there was an internal struggle within Jimmy about that, probably because, simply, his own dad had always been the breadwinner.

When we had children, that pressure increased exponentially on Jimmy, mostly because by then, I'd given up my secure job and I'd been working in the music industry for three years. As I mentioned earlier, falling pregnant meant I was unceremoniously dumped from the music industry as a touring production assistant and tour manager, so I was bringing in almost nothing financially. We had also just bought our first house, so paying the mortgage was, obviously, a big deal to both of us. My approach to money has always been, 'It'll be fine,' mostly because it always had been fine. I can see now, I didn't really acknowledge my privilege that stood as the basis for that belief. I had parents who were well-off and, honestly, part of me knew that they'd never see us homeless. Jimmy didn't have the same privileged outlook and the fear about not having enough money to sustain a house and a family was a very real one for him.

It was only during couples' therapy that he gave a voice to his own version of the mental load for the first time. While I was drowning in postnatal depression and nurturing all my resentments about being a solo parent for most of the year, Jimmy was desperately trying to do everything he could to keep a roof over our heads. My self-centred fear about what kind of mother I was and how my life had changed and how I'd lost myself, meant that I didn't stop to consider that Jimmy wasn't away by choice. It didn't occur to me that he'd rather be home with us, helping in a more hands-on way, spending time with his daughter in her first year. I was too angry about the fact that he could get a full night's sleep in a five-star hotel and sun himself on the beaches around the world on his days off to ever think about the fact that he was desperately trying to make sure he could pay all the bills. And it wasn't like he was a banker or a doctor. Jimmy had done the impossible and was managing to make a decent living as a musician – he had become a well-respected session musician touring with the likes of George Ezra, Dido, Bryan Ferry, Mika and many more – but it came with sacrifices of a kind I didn't have the capacity to consider at the time, struggling as I was.

I must earn enough money, was the constant ticker tape that ran through his head along with, *I need to be home more, I'm not present for my daughter, my wife isn't doing well, I can't be in two places at once, I have to be on the ball for every show, I'm worried about what's going on at home, I need to look after myself, I need to look after my wife and daughter, I need to look after the bills.* It's not the same list that women deal with but it's a list of impossibilities nonetheless, and that takes its toll, too.

The moral of this chapter takes me back to the quote at the beginning of it. *Good men and women do exist but sometimes you have to stop focusing on what's wrong with them and start looking for what's right.* I spent so much time and energy looking for what was wrong with Jimmy in terms of how he was or wasn't providing for my needs, and not enough time or energy considering whether I was even conscious of his. How much of the mental load was to make me feel better rather than to support him in a way that was meaningful according to his own pressures? Yes, he needed to step up and share my mental load with me but, in return, the very least I could do was take a hot minute to acknowledge his and consider that maybe, *just maybe*, I wasn't the only one in the relationship who needed a little bit of empathy, support and compassion.

22

Nurture *Not* Nature

When I initially decided to write this chapter, I wanted to
interview people in single-sex relationships, transgender men
and women, couples from different cultures and religions and
socio-economic backgrounds. I wanted to see how men and
women from every corner of existence managed the mental
load and how the expectation of people in relationships
changed when you placed the lens of intersectionality over
them. I wanted to learn as much as I could and then make
it clear to you, the reader, that I wasn't lacking self-awareness,
that I wasn't just another obnoxious, middle-class, white
woman, trading on her privilege and telling my story as if it
was the only one.

I gravitate towards managing the home and all that entails
because that's what I saw my mum do. I'm a girl and therefore the message was subliminal but very clear: this is what
you will also do. But what I really wanted to know was – is
it *really* all down to gender? And, if it is, is it because women
are genetically woven together and naturally inclined to base
themselves in the home, or is it all socially enforced upon us?
Is it, essentially, nature or nurture?

Do women bear a disproportionate percentage of the mental load because we are, quite simply, women – nothing more, nothing less? Is our superior ability to multitask an inherent feminine skill? A gene that men don't possess and therefore can't be expected to utilise? We assume that it is our XX chromosome that means we are *built* to manage a multitude of tasks all at once. Somewhere, at some point in the evolution of the human race, we have unquestioningly accepted that the responsibility of keeping our own domestic worlds running smoothly falls on us because, as the female of the species, we are inherently designed to do so.

Throughout the ages, society has always been keen to create narratives for women and present them as true. Think about every woman in a Jane Austen novel. Women are inherently prone to flights of fancy, fainting spells, exhaustion and madness. There's no question that this is a social construct. Women just *are* weak and fragile beings who must be handled firmly and directed clearly by, of course, a man or two – usually a father and a husband. Throughout history, women have been forced to exist in these false realities; we have been coerced into accepting our ineptitude as a given, our sexuality as a curse, our folds and curves as unacceptable, our intellect as being only suitable for casseroles and darning.

If you're a woman and you've ever said the words, *men can't multitask*, then I hate to say it, but the patriarchy has got you exactly where it wants you to be. And you're not the only one. I've said those words many times and truly believed them to be true. In some ways, I think I wanted that stereotype and others like it to be true so that I could justify the lack of support I felt or the lack of willingness on the part of the man who supposedly loved me, to help me. It was another way of saying, *He would if he could, bless him*.

But all of that is true, only if you believe that we are, at a cellular level – at the level of *nature* – predisposed as women to deal with the admin of life and family, and I don't think we need to do extensive scientific research to recognise that as bullshit. There is no *nature* when it comes to the mental load and which gender is 'better' at managing it. It's all fucking nurture. All of it. Every last sodding drop of the expectation that women should be responsible for the domestic graft is less biological and more bloody illogical. It is misogyny run wild. It is the patriarchy oppressing the matriarchy. It is men making women do what they don't want to. When it comes down to it, it's that fucking simple. And before someone starts yelling, *It's not all men*, don't bother, because actually, on some level, it is all men. It's not all their *fault*. We can't hold individual men responsible for the gargantuan prison that a man-made society has created, but we can encourage those individual men to recognise it as their responsibility to dismantle it brick by brick.

The first thing I did when I started to write this chapter was google: *Is there a culture or community in the world where men are responsible for the domestic work?* The short answer is, unsurprisingly, 'no'. The longer answer went something like this:

While no single culture universally places the majority of domestic work solely on men, some cultures and communities are moving towards a more equal division of household [labour], with men taking on a significantly larger role in domestic tasks, particularly in Scandinavian countries like Sweden and Norway where gender equality is highly valued; however, even in these regions, traditional gender roles still influence domestic work to some extent[6]

It felt like the natural place to start would be to interview people in same-sex relationships. What happens when you take the gender variation out of the experiment? On whose shoulders does the mental load rest when two men share a life together? How is the labour divided when two women are married or in a relationship? Social norms would suggest that a same-sex male couple should be living in chaos, with no clean laundry, while a house belonging to a same-sex female couple should be hyper-organised, efficient, and spotlessly clean. Right? Wrong.

Vin is a very good friend of mine. He's in his fifties, although he looks annoyingly young. He's a vegan, a musician, and probably one of the nicest people I know. He's married to Mark – also in his fifties, also irritatingly young-looking (I suppose that's what happens when you're childfree, not sleep-deprived and have disposable income). They've been together for almost thirty years and, like anyone in a long-term relationship, they have grown to understand each other in a way that only living with someone for thirty years can allow you to. They look at each other unfiltered – they've seen the ugliest corners of each other's souls and lovingly accept them even if they don't always like them. This is a marriage that I see as aspirational. It's also one of the most solid I know *not* because of its perfection, but because of its imperfections.

I started by asking Vin what the term 'mental load' meant to him.

'It's basically the person who just takes the responsibility, particularly for the domestic situation,' he replies. 'But, it's not who necessarily *does* jobs, it's who takes the responsibility for deciding when they get done, and whether they get done, and whether they remember it, and writes it in the calendar, or makes it happen. It's that person.'

At this moment, I just want to take a minute to acknowledge the point that Vin makes. It's not just the *doing* of the task. It's the planning for that task. It's the trying not to forget that something needs doing. It's the getting everything you need to make that task happen and then, more often than not, it culminates in the doing of it because you're the one that's done all the thinking about it. The act of *doing* the task is not what we're struggling with as women – or not the *only* thing we are struggling with – it's all the other stuff that comes with it. All the other drop-down menus that suddenly appear when someone says something as simple as, 'We should have them over for dinner,' because for the one managing the mental load, it's never that simple.

We should have them over for dinner ...

Check everyone's schedules and organise a date
that works for everyone

Clean the house

Plan a meal and do a supermarket shop
(Allergies? Meat?)

Make sure the bathroom is clean

Plan that day so I have time to cook and prepare

Wash hair the night before

But I digress. I asked Vin who was responsible for all that stuff, for all the drop-down menus in their life.

'It's really interesting,' he says thoughtfully. 'As soon as you asked me about this, I started analysing our relationship and wondering who is responsible for that stuff. I'm sure Mark thinks he's got the mental load of things and I think that I do, but I think over the years, the various responsibilities have just been divvied up naturally'.

'So,' I respond, 'what you're saying is that the mental load and the domestic labour is fairly evenly distributed?'

'Oh no,' Vin says quickly. 'I'm not saying that at all.'

We talk at length about how Vin sees himself as the bearer of the mental load. When they moved in together, he took responsibility for buying the house, organising the mortgage, managing the move, designing the house. He sorted the insurance for the subsidence, he bought the things, organised the delivery, the tradespeople when required, and he did a lot of the work himself.

'I remember one time very clearly. I came home from work, went upstairs to get changed out of my work clothes and into clothes I did DIY in, came downstairs and got straight onto working on the house while Mark sat on the sofa watching TV. For two weeks, I decorated the whole house and he sat and watched telly. There was definitely a resentment there.'

By Vin's own admission, he'd accept that he's a people-pleaser and that he's struggled with feeling responsible for making sure others are happy and that their wants and needs are met, sometimes to the detriment of his own. I think it's a quality most women who find themselves the default architect and maintenance woman for the lives of their family members can relate to. But why Vin? Why, when it comes to taking that responsibility, or perhaps accepting that responsibility in a male–male relationship, was it Vin who grabbed hold of it with both hands and not Mark?

'That's quite a complicated question, isn't it?' Vin replies. 'Mark doesn't like confrontation, so rather than get involved and find himself in a disagreement over something, he just sits back and I take control. And . . .' – Vin hesitates for a second – 'I guess on some level, I want the credit too. That's a big admission.'

It really is, and one that impresses me. It also hits me hard because I have to admit that there are definitely times when

I want the credit too. Sure, some of that is about yearning for the appreciation that I deserve, but most of it is about martyring myself a little, too.

'It's also to do with my own personal history,' Vin continues. 'My childhood. My father died when I was ten and I didn't actually spend a lot of time with him when he was alive because he was at work most of the time. There were four of us kids and I was the youngest. My mum went out to work and my two older brothers did fuck all because they weren't expected to help. My sister, though, was the one who had to cook the dinner and do the housework while Mum worked, and because I was the closest to her in age – I was basically her doll – I had a huge sense of loyalty to her because it all felt so unfair. So I did everything she did; I helped her clean the house and cook dinner.'

This lands heavily between us because, of course, it makes perfect sense. While Vin is obviously a man, he spent his formative years helping his sister manage a good deal of the mental load in his childhood home. He was up close and personal with it. He saw the mental load and the unpaid labour that women do all day, every day, and so, of course, when it comes to divvying up the responsibility in his adult relationships, he gravitates to what he knows, what he grew up seeing and doing. Inadvertently, he was caught in the crosshairs of social norms. Nurture *not* nature.

I also interviewed Nicola, a mum who's been in a relationship with wife Anna for seventeen years. They have two children, Tabitha (8) and Daniel (5), and with that comes the usual day-to-day brain noise that we all associate with a 2.4 family. I was intrigued to know, in a female–female relationship, whether it was a bit like that time I went on holiday with a friend of mine and our kids. Both of our husbands were away with work, so one Easter we booked an Airbnb. And let me tell you: it was glorious. I'd be giving the kids breakfast and I'd look up to find my friend making sarnies for lunch and collecting and filling up water bottles . . . *all without being asked*! After dinner, I'd be loading the dishwasher while my friend put the kids in the bath and did a clean-up so that we didn't have to sit surrounded by the detritus of the day as we watched *Married at First Sight*. I asked Nicola if her marriage was one long Easter Airbnb.

'No,' she laughs. 'I'll walk into a room and say, "This place is such a mess," and she'll be like, "Why? What's wrong with it?" There will be at least seven pieces of random clothing discarded around the room, on the backs of sofas, the floor, you know, and I'll think, *How can you not see it?*'

So far, so relatable.

'And we're both femme,' Nicola explains. 'My friend told me to make sure you knew that we're both femme – neither of us are butch, so it's nothing to do with that.'

I don't want to put words in Nicola's mouth, but I think the assumption is that this would be more easily explained if one of them was 'butch' and therefore more masculine, but here, that's not the case. Having learned what I've learned, however, I'm not even sure that's true.

'So,' I push, 'why is that? Why are you the one that sees it and she doesn't?'

Nicola considers this carefully. 'As we're talking about it now, it's just the way it's cascaded down through the generations. You know? As women, we tend to watch our mums, and in Anna's family, her mum isn't the cleaner or the tidier; it's her dad.'

Huh. So, while Vin was, as a man, over-exposed relatively to the traditionally female role of mental load bearer in his house, Anna, Nicola's wife, was exposed to a partnership that bucked traditional trends. It wasn't that she was somehow aligned more closely to the traditionally masculine role in a relationship, it's that her parents had already turned traditional roles on their head and, in her family, the feminine role wasn't the cleaner or the tidier or the organiser.

Anna's parents' set-up seems radical, especially considering they're part of the Boomer generation. I mention this.

'Well, my father-in-law was raised pretty intentionally by his mum. His father couldn't do anything and I think she wanted to make sure her son didn't end up the same way. So, by the time he left home she made sure he could iron, he could cook, he could sew – he could do all the things he needed to do.'

Not rocket science by any stretch, but shocking nonetheless, because I've mentioned a few times in this book that so much of the unequal division of labour in a relationship is down to what we are implicitly or directly told is our job as a woman or a man. I've talked about how, consciously or not, girls are taught how to iron, how to clean a bathroom, how to cook, and men are taught that they need to earn money and, if they want to be really generous with their time, they could take the bins out . . . if they're not too tired. In Anna's father's case, he was *very* consciously taught the lessons that were normally reserved for little girls and the results were clear: he was able to do all those things that society tells us women are better suited for. Nurture *not* nature.

I think this is positive. For those of us – men and women – who want to change the way society pigeonholes women, for the way it holds us back by keeping us tethered to the mental load, this seems to suggest that the solution, while not easy, is seemingly simple. All it takes is a conscious veering away from traditional gender roles when it comes to how we parent and, if I'm honest, it's the little boys we are letting down. For many years now, we have all been encouraged to challenge those social norms traditionally placed on little girls. Lego now comes in pretty colours (it's a mixed message, admittedly, but a start nonetheless). We openly talk about how girls should have a seat at every table, not just the ones they furnish with food and wipe down afterwards. We tell them they're strong, capable and able to have it all, but unless the boys they are going to grow up and live with aren't freed from their own set of social norms, it's more of a curse than a blessing.

If we want women to *really* have access to the world in its entirety, with no limitations, then we need to deprogram boys from associating the domestic workload with emasculation. It's not enough that little girls are encouraged to think beyond the front doors of their immaculate houses if little boys aren't encouraged to look after it while they're gone. And, if Vin's and Nicola's stories are anything to go by, it could be as simple as making sure little boys look to their mums as role models and that the men in their life encourage them to do that too.

23

Becoming Bilingual

'The husband decides he will motivate his wife to become more respectful by acting in unloving ways. This usually proves about as successful as trying to sell a pickup to an Amish farmer. Unfortunately, a wife's usual approach is to complain and criticize in order to motivate her husband to become more loving. This usually proves about as successful as trying to sell brass knuckles to Mother Teresa.'
– Dr Emerson Eggerichs, *Love and Respect: The Love She Most Desires; The Respect He Desperately Needs*

I haven't read the book *Men Are from Mars, Women Are from Venus*, but as metaphors go, the title seems pretty spot on. Another book I've also not read, but feel like I have due to its insemination into the zeitgeist, is *The Five Love Languages*, which are defined as touch, words of affirmation, service, gifts and time. What these books and many others like it – including this one – tell us is that not only is it likely that, on a general level, men and women approach life differently, but that they also speak different languages when it comes to interacting with each other and showing love and respect.

What this means is that we are at risk of forgetting this and making the assumption that everyone approaches life like we do and speaks the same language we do. I spent a long time making that mistake. I also went one step further and believed that the way I approach life and the language I speak are inherently *right*. This inflexibility all came from a place of fear – I had to be right, I had to do things the way I wanted to do them because if I didn't, they wouldn't be perfect and that would prove that I was, actually, when you got down to brass tacks, a useless human.

It's never clearer that men and women, of our generation especially,★ are from different planets than when it comes to navigating the mental load of life together. I've talked about this extensively, but regarding the things we were taught while growing up, the things we were told were our responsibility, whether directly or implicitly, men and women may as well have been raised on opposite ends of the Milky Way. Accepting that fact was key to my understanding of why Jimmy and I could not get on the same page when it came to managing the mental load. I was expecting him to immediately understand what I'd spent my whole life learning. For the generations before us, that wasn't really a problem because men and women accepted their roles. Millennials, though, have the unasked-for honour of being the cycle breakers, and we can only do that if we are willing to concede that there is a disconnect with the world we find ourselves living in versus the world we were all trained to live in back in the day. As they say, the first step to recovery is accepting you

★ I'm referring to Millennials, the offspring of Boomers.

have a problem and, Houston, we have a problem. All of us. Men and women. No one is particularly happy with the way things are.

When you're feeling unsupported, unheard, unrecognised and unappreciated, it's really difficult to go beyond those feelings and consider what the other person might be feeling. It's even harder to stop focusing on what they did to make you feel that way and what your part in it might be. Add to that the fact that you speak different 'love languages' and you're both so concerned with the feeling that they don't understand you, that you forget to consider they may also be frustrated that *you* don't understand *them*.

Here's the secret that I've learned that no one tells you: even if both of you are mega efficient and organised when it comes to the mental load, you're still never going to get on top of it. It's still going to feel stressful and overwhelming, because there's no finish line to it. You don't defeat it, you don't get a medal, you don't get to stand on a podium, waving while people cheer you for being the best at the mental load. So, if we can accept that it's a never-ending task, no matter what, then the only question that matters is this: do you want to work your way through the never-ending to do list with someone who you like and respect, who likes and respects you? Someone who listens to you because you can communicate calmly and honestly and who you listen to because you know that, despite any mistakes or fuck-ups, they've got your best interests at heart? Or do you want to go through it fighting, feeling like you're on your own and rotting with resentment?

I learned that while I was controlling everything, the latter was the only possible option. If my expectations were the only 'right' ones, if my standards were the only acceptable ones and if my priorities had to be everyone else's priorities, then fighting my way through domestic life was my only option. I had no idea how inflexible I was nor how double my standards were.

For example, I wanted Jimmy to load the dishwasher in a certain way. The way I loaded it meant you could fit more in and everything got clean. Sure, it took a little more time and care to do it, but it was worth it. Every time he didn't do it my way, I would feel that familiar rage seep throughout my body. The rage wasn't about the dishwasher; the rage was because of the coded message I received as a result of his decision to load the dishwasher in a less than optimal way, despite being asked a million times. The message was this: *I don't give a shit about what she wants, I'm going to do it my way. If she wants it doing her way, then she should do it herself. She should be grateful I'm doing it at all.* To be clear, this isn't what Jimmy *ever* actually said to me. This is just what I interpreted from his actions.

My feelings here are valid, but what I wasn't doing was considering my part in this deal. Jimmy does all the bins, not because he's a man, but because I wretch when I get near mould, bad smells and sticky garbage. I cannot count the amount of times I have just chucked big boxes in the general direction of the bin for him to deal with. I have, at times, been a world champion in Bin Jenga – you know, when, rather than take the bins out, you just keep piling the rubbish on until it's all Trash Tower, balancing precariously? He's asked me a million times to break down the boxes so that they take up less space in recycling and for years I didn't do it because of a sort of 'it's the least he can do' mentality. *I do everything else . . . it's the least he can do.*

Sure, there's probably some truth to that on a factual level, but we aren't factual creatures. We are emotional ones, and if I feel disrespected when he doesn't take the time to load the dishwasher properly, then of course he's going to feel the same way when I don't break down the boxes, or when I just keep piling rubbish on top of rubbish. Now, when a parcel arrives in a big box, I grab the box-cutter and take five minutes to cut it up into smaller pieces that will fit efficiently in the recycling bin. It's annoying, sure, but it's just my attempt to show him that I understand his love language and I'm learning to speak it too.

I think women are at risk of holding the moral high ground hostage when it comes to the mental load. The advantage is in our court. We've got a millennia's worth of evidence to support how badly treated women have been in domestic spaces and male–female relationships and so it's easy to weaponise that and use it against the men of our generation. But, if we're not going to stand for their weaponised incompetence, then we also can't weaponise our trauma and beat them over the head with it.

It's easy for us to mock, criticise, humiliate the men in our lives when it comes to what may seem like domestic ineptitude, but if they were to do the same to us in return, there would be outrage. I've been responsible for enabling and encouraging that attitude with many, many videos on social media that mock my husband all in the name of comedy. And don't get me wrong, they are funny, but there's also an underlying unkindness there and it took me way longer than it should have done to recognise that. While those observations may have been accurate, using them to highlight his crappy household habits wasn't an efficient tactic for getting him to change them. And it doesn't matter if you're posting them on social media or not. Sarcastic comments in front of other people, eye-rolls behind his back when he asks a 'stupid' question or criticising him in social situations are things we've all been guilty of, but I realised I had to stop if I actually wanted things to change.

They say that nothing changes if nothing changes and that's painfully accurate when it comes to managing the mental load. We didn't just inherit the responsibility of the mental load from our mothers, we also inherited the resentments and the emotionally inept way of dealing with them. Forgive me, Boomer mums, I know your pain was never even recognised, let alone given the space to be aired, but the silent treatment, the tutting, the door slamming and the shouting matches were tried and tested and found wanting, and yet I relied on those tactics for many years.

Doing things differently requires humility and vulnerability. I had to admit that my way wasn't the only way. I had to admit that my expectations were unreasonable and unattainable. I had to admit – and this might have been the hardest thing – that I couldn't do it all. I had to be open to the idea that Jimmy may have something useful to say in how the house was run and managed, even though everything I'd learned growing up went against that. The fact that men were useless in the home was sold to me as an intractable fact rather than a myth designed to make us all laugh condescendingly rather than confront the truth: that we all felt powerless in a domestic situation that was making us miserable.

So, I guess the moral of this particular story is that we need to start speaking each other's language. We have to become bilingual in our relationships rather than demand that everyone else learns and speaks our preferred language.

24

When the Exception
Proves the Rule

'We cannot continue down this path of violence against women when we know it is preventable and it is based on respect and equality for women.' – Patty Kinnersly, CEO, Our Watch

Perhaps the real reason that we so often, as women, point to the mental load and the devastating effects it has on women around the world is because in a lot of ways it's the tip of the inequality iceberg. Maybe its prominence in the zeitgeist is because it's an easily identifiable symbol of the inequality between men and women that still pervades our society. If you're reading this in a Western culture, amid the trappings of a household that is, to all intents and purposes, safe, then you are one of the lucky ones. If your biggest issue is that you don't feel kept in mind by your partner, then as crappy as that can feel, relatively speaking, you're doing okay. You still have the power of choice. I'm not saying you should suck it up and be grateful, but I do think perspective and awareness of our privilege is important in any situation.

I couldn't finish this book without acknowledging that for

every one of us struggling with the negative mental and relational consequences that are a result of the unequal distribution of the mental load, there is another woman feeling, in a very literal and a very violent sense, the more extreme consequences of a society that doesn't value women. It's all part of the same problem and there are no grey areas when it comes to this topic. If *any* formal or informal inequality between men and women continues to exist, and is *allowed* to exist, then women will always live, to a greater or lesser extent, in fear of men. No matter how small the chink in the armour of equality, there will always be men who will find that vulnerability and exploit it.

According to the European Institute for Gender Equality, 'Gender-based violence is a phenomenon deeply rooted in gender inequality, and continues to be one of the most notable human rights violations within all societies.'[6] When the women of Iceland took to the streets and went on strike once again in 2023, they reiterated their call for pay equality but also added action on gender-based violence to their demands too. The link between a socially embedded gender inequality and violence towards women has been well proven in recent years.

Violence against women is not, and should never be considered, an inevitable result of men and women sharing space in society, but unless you have experienced it, it's easy to forget the connection between accepting what may seem like harmless or even privileged inequalities and violence against women and girls. While women in violent relationships are the exception to the advice I've clumsily imparted in this book, they are also what proves the rule, because violence against women is both a cause and a consequence of gender inequality. It is something we can no longer shy away from. If a man is unwilling to hear you, to recognise your role in the world as valid and valued, then it's worryingly easy to see how that disregard can turn into derision and ultimately into violence. It's all part of the same problem. It all sits on the same spectrum.

So, while I hope this book has helped the majority of us who have very valid but very non-violent struggles within our relationship, I also hope that it serves to highlight the more sinister consequences of a world where women are considered inherently less-than. Sure, there are things we can laugh about and there are jokes to be made around the audacity of men when it comes to the mental load, but that can't be at the exclusion of the much more important discussion around violence against women and girls. And yes, I know, it's not all men, but here's the problem: we don't know *which* men it is, and so, in order to protect ourselves, women inevitably assume, on some level, that it is all men, or, at least, it could be.

25

Final Thoughts

When I started to write this book, I was very clear that I didn't want it to be a self-help book. I have no credentials. I am an expert in absolutely nothing. There is no world where I should be allowed to write a book that, in any way, shape or form, tries to tell others what to do. Sure, I can share a few tips and tricks that worked for me and Jimmy, but the only thing I really know how to do is to share my own experience – the good, the bad and the ugly. Because, after years and years of (over)sharing my own experiences, I've come to understand the value in it.

In recent years, almost all the content I've put out there, be it in books, podcasts or on social media, has always been about sharing my own experiences so that others can feel encouraged to share theirs. When that happens, the space we create between my experience and yours is often a safe one, and in a world where safe spaces are few and far between, that is not to be taken for granted.

I don't believe the art of telling stories – fictional or not – came to exist for entertainment, at least not initially. Back in the day, I don't think the cave people painted pictorial tales on the walls of their caves in the blood of a captured hare to get a laugh, or to scare someone, or to make someone cry. They did it, I believe to *share*. Those stories, and all the stories since, have been gifted to us by people willing to share their internal world with the external. The stories we tell at the pub, on the phone, on the internet, are a little piece of ourselves that we offer up as a tiny representation of who we are and why we are. Each one of those stories, once out in the world, spools from us like a thread so that other people can hold on to them and tie their own similar stories to them. It is in the telling of stories that we are able to connect. It is in that connection that we experience a stability, a grounding.

Some people go to church to hear stories they can connect with, that help them feel grounded. Some people go to the gym. Some people listen to podcasts, or join choirs, or go on wellness retreats. Some people go to 12-step meetings, some people join cults, or volunteer for charities. At some level, all our interactions with other people stem from an inherent and vital human need to share our own stories and therefore build connections with people with whom they have a shared experience.

There were things in this book that I wondered whether or not I should include, but in the end, there was very little I took out. If I did take things out, it was because the legal team told me I should or because it wasn't my story to tell. It was important to me that the deeply shameful stuff that I would have liked, in all honesty, to take to my grave, was in here. I knew that it was important to share the very worst of me because it helped to authenticate all the other stories too. As they say, there are no lies here. Perhaps there are some misrememberings, perhaps a version of the truth, my version, but no lies.

As women, we have developed our own way of sharing stories to help us survive a world we often feel excluded from. We get together for lunch, coffee or a bottle or two of wine and we talk about all the things we're struggling with. We tell stories of our husbands and their bad behaviour and we use those stories to bond and connect. We can be tempted to gossip about people when they're not in the room, and use those stories, as accurate or inaccurate as they may be, to make ourselves feel better. I often think that the conversations we have with our girlfriends about the men in our lives are the ones we should probably be having with the men in our lives. Instead, we seem to save a more reflective, thoughtful approach for a discussion with our girlfriends and go on the attack when it comes to tackling the same issue with our partners.

I also want to acknowledge how lucky we are as women to have what appears to be an instinctive inclination towards connection. While toxic masculinity has done women dirty, it's also screwed the good men over too. Men have never been given permission to talk about their feelings with each other in the same way that women have. It makes me sad that, in general, men don't have the same culture, the same outlet, with which to share stories and therefore feel connected. They don't tend to play golf and talk about their feelings, and when they get drunk, it's more likely to end up in a boisterous display of masculinity, rather than an intense D&M (if you're too young to know what a D&M is, read the footnote).*

---

* D&M: deep and meaningful. Usage: 'Give us a minute, darling, Helen and I are in the middle of a D&M.'

Many men don't have anyone to talk to about how they are feeling in their relationship and I can only imagine how lonely it might be to believe you're the only one that doesn't feel like a good husband, or the only one who feels unheard by their partner. For many men, the only person they are comfortable opening up to are their female partners, but when their relationship with that female partner is the thing they need to talk about, where do they go?

Maybe part of building effective communication with our partners is about encouraging them to open up to friends, to build those connections and find those safe spaces. I think men can feel pretty isolated and left alone with their anxieties, worries and fears, and I don't think that helps the dynamic. Maybe encouraging the men in our lives to open up to their friends will show them they're not on their own and that marital discord isn't a personal failing or evidence of defective manliness.

In the meantime, I want to thank you for reading this book. I want to thank you for taking the time to hear my story because while I hope there was something in this book that helped you, it's not an entirely selfless endeavour. From readers of the book, I know I will receive emails and messages from women (and hopefully men!) about how it helped them feel less alone. You will share your own stories with me in response and those stories will, in turn, help me feel less alone. So, thank you.

Finally, to all the people out there who feel overwhelmingly normal in a world peppered with major and minor celebrities and anyone with a platform, please know that the gloss and the glamour is all nonsense. If you've followed me on social media, you'll know that the gloss and glamour is not that plentiful, but I know I am guilty of sometimes serving up the shiny bits and calling it real life. It's not real life. As I write this, my kids are crying because they're tired and they can't have McDonald's. One of them has just thrown the remote across the room. The other one broke my laptop this morning. I'm freezing cold because my husband won't let me put the heating on because, apparently, I'm not wearing enough clothes. He is also annoyed because we've both got colds and even though we both feel like a bag of donkey bollocks, he has to take care of the kids because I have a book deadline, so I get to lock myself in my office and absent myself of all responsibility, while I sip warm tea and have a little nap every three hours or so. We have recycling piled up in the front hall and the garden because we missed the recycling bin collection a month ago and we've never managed to get back on track. There's a parcel that needs to go to the post office. It's been sitting on the stairs for three weeks. My bed sheets haven't been changed in a fortnight, there's a load of laundry in the washing machine that I've forgotten to take out and washed twice now and if I even start thinking about the fact that the garden fence needs replacing, the front yard needs weeding and power washing, the hallway and stairs need painting, the dog needs bathing, the uniform needs ironing and an Instagram reel or two needs making, I might just have a panic attack.

Instead, I'm trying to ignore the persistent twitching in my left eye and the whispers of an oncoming headache and focus on the fact that I am, in fact, about to finish writing my book – the very book you are reading now. I'm going to take a minute to wallow in the joy of my childhood dream of being an author coming true and congratulate myself for making it happen. Today, it's a book. I know, that sounds very lofty and deeply unrelatable, but tomorrow, my biggest achievement might just be getting through the day without losing my shit. It's all relative.

So, if you're stuck in the exhausting cycle of rage, repair, repeat when it comes to managing the mental load, please know that you're not the only one. The world is an exhausting place to navigate, especially when you have to consider the feelings, thoughts, wants and needs of others – the audacity!

I hope this book – my story – has provided a few threads for you to hold on to, a safe space for you to have helpful discussions and a feeling that we are all connected. At the very least, I hope this book provides even just a little bit of comfort to those of you who feel at your wits' end as a woman in this world.

We *all* know what that feels like.

Cat

EPILOGUE

The Mental Load List
that Went Viral

'For all those men who say, "Why buy the cow when you can get the milk for free?", here's an update for you. Nowadays 80% of women are against marriage. Why? Because women realize it's not worth buying an entire pig just to get a little sausage!' – Frank Kaiser

Back in early 2022, I created The Mental Load List. The idea came from a conversation my husband and I had one day. I'm sure it followed yet another loss of shit on my part about the state of the house and the mental load and blah, blah, blah. You get the idea. My husband came up to me afterwards and said, with nothing but a genuine desire to understand, 'Tell me what the mental load is. I don't know if I understand it and I really want to.' I could have got indignant and self-righteous and got in my own way by telling him that he was old enough and ugly enough to figure it out himself, but I didn't. Instead, I took him at his word, gave him the benefit of the doubt, and set to trying to explain it.

The problem was, that no matter how many examples I gave of the kind of things that make up the mental load, the things that clatter through our brain like a marching band playing five different songs all at the same time, nothing seemed to truly convey the enormity of it, the weightiness of it. So, ever the writer, I decided to try to write it all down.

I spent the next two days writing lists upon lists of any and every thing I've ever known to make up part of the mental load. I organised it by rooms in the house, key life events, general life admin, scheduling and a million other sectors I could think of that I appeared to have inherited responsibility for. It ended up being forty-seven pages long and when I put it on sale as a digital download for £8 on my website, www.notsosmugnow.com, it made over £3,000 in the first forty-eight hours. It continues to sell well today. It was written about on news outlets around the world. *Grazia* asked me to write an article about it. The content I made about it on social media had millions and millions of views across Instagram, TikTok and Facebook. It hit a nerve in the way that very few things a writer writes ever does and eventually, and unsurprisingly, it led to Simon & Schuster offering me a deal to turn it into a book – the book you are reading now.

And so, I include The Mental Load List here. For those of you who already bought it, this is a somewhat updated and refined version. For those of you who haven't purchased it previously – there's no need now. What follows is the most comprehensive list in existence of the thousands of items that fly through our heads on a daily basis. These are as many of the tasks I could possibly think of, that we have learned to habitually manage at significant cost to our relationships, our careers and our mental and physical health. Somehow, seeing them all written down in one space seems to have been the therapy many of us needed. I hope it helps you as much as it helped me. In turn, I hope it helps you convey to your partners the gargantuan nature of a job that, within any corporation, would elicit an enormous salary rate but that we, as women, do for free, day in and day out.

Endnotes

1 Pg. 96 'The day the women went on strike', Annadis Rudolfsdottir, *Guardian*, 18 October 2005.

2 Pg. 96 'Icelandic women strike for economic and social equality, 1975 | Global Nonviolent Action Database', Global Nonviolent Action Database, Swarthmore College. Retrieved 23 April 2016.

3 Pg. 113 https://www.addictioncenter.com/addiction/differences-men-women/

4 Pg. 209 Solane Bramhill, *The Comparison Trap: Social Media and Mental Health envy.*' https://carleton.ca/pmc/2024/the-comparison-trap-social-media-and-mental-health/

5 Pg. 210 https://www.oberlo.com/statistics/social-media-usage-by-gender

6 Pg. 251 https://eige.europa.eu/gender-based-violence/what-is-gender-based-violence?language_content_entity=en#:~:text=Gender%2Dbased%20violence%20is%20a,person%20because%20of%20their%20gender.

Acknowledgements

In some ways it feels wildly unfair that it's only my name on the spine of this book. What I've come to learn is that it takes a village to write a book, and without my village, this book would never have come to fruition.

The biggest shout-out has to go to my wonderful literary agent, the inimitable Anna Dixon at YMU. I know we agreed that this was going to be a *very* professional relationship but somewhere along the line you have become one of my most trusted friends. It's just a bonus that you're also one of the most impressive people I've ever had the pleasure of working with. The question *What would Anna do?* is one I ask myself regularly. I'm sorry I cried in public when you said you wanted to represent me and I'm sorry you have to text me to tell me to pick up the damn phone and that I'm not in trouble because you know that my default expectation is that everyone is always cross with me for something. Your patience with me and my constant anxieties must warrant some kind of medal, but I hope this acknowledgement will suffice. I hope this is the first of many projects we create together.

Thank you to Michelle Signore at Simon & Schuster who

took a punt on me when others chose not to. You were the first person to truly get what I wanted to do with this book. You knew it wasn't a self-help book, that it wasn't going to offer any solutions, but that its flex was the relatability and the reassurance for readers that they're not on their own with the mental load and all the problems it throws up. There's a comfort in reading a story you relate to and I wanted this book, more than anything, to be comforting. I'm not sure there was a Self Help-Comedy-Memoir category before, but between us we've carved one out!

Thanks also to Alison and Maudisa at Simon & Schuster and Victoria, my copyeditor, for your close reading of the manuscript to make it as good as it possibly could be. Thank you for picking up on every repetition, every unclear sentence, every typo, grammatical error and nonsensical phrase. You all have an attention to detail that I will never be capable of and am eternally jealous of. Thank you also to Justine at Simon & Schuster for the marketing and promotion of this book.

Huge love and thanks must also go to Katie Ray (and everyone at Radient Management) for being the best manager a girl could have. Your support and kindness have been unwavering, and knowing that I've got you in my corner has been life-changing. I know I'm not easy to manage – I'm pretty chaotic, always working on something new, rarely finishing anything on time and rubbish at responding to WhatsApps – but I never, ever take you and all the hard work you do behind the scenes for granted. Thank you, my darling.

To my friends – Cherry Healey, Mika Simmons, Reagan Kempton, Anna Whitehouse, Cat Rosenthal, Emma Nicolet, Charlie Brooks, Ciara Janson, Anna Hristou and Michelle

Righini, who have read passages and sent me encouraging notes and helpful suggestions, who have put up with me banging on about the mental load, who have answered all my questions as I 'researched' (a term I use very loosely) the book, who have encouraged me when I was pretty sure I'd be better off burning the whole manuscript, who have been on the end of the phone, partnered me on walks through the woods, picked up my kids when I had a deadline and couldn't get there – you're all cracking human beings and I'm lucky to have you in my life.

Special thanks as well to Vin Goodwin and Nicola Smithson-Brook for agreeing to be interviewed about your relationships and how you manage the mental load in your own lives. You were both so open and honest. Thank you for giving up your time. Thanks as well to Alli Scott – I finished this book in your beautiful barn. Your hosting was second to none, and I will be back when I don't have a deadline looming!

To every single one of my followers on Instagram, TikTok, Threads, Substack and everywhere else . . . a truly heartfelt thank you. None of this would have happened if you hadn't shown your faith in me as a creator and writer by hitting that little Follow button. It may seem like a small thing, worth nothing, but like many small things, together they become very powerful. While I hope my writing stands on its own merit, I'm also aware that my following opened doors and gave me opportunities which otherwise may not have been available to me. That's all because of you – so thank you, truly.

To my gorgeous mama – Pam. I don't know whether you'll ever read this book or whether the Parkinson's will have taken that from you, but please know that I get it now. I'm so sorry that there were times when you didn't feel heard, seen, supported or respected. I'm sorry I was angry for a long time and I'm sorry I didn't stop to see your point of view earlier. I'm not the only kid who forgot their parents are human, but I see it now and I love you for all your hard work and sacrifices. My love for you is endless.

Dad, I wouldn't be a writer if it wasn't for you. You're probably the only dad who, when it came to bedtime stories, made me read *your* book to you. By the time I was ten, I'd read John le Carré's *Tinker, Tailor, Soldier, Spy* from cover to cover. I didn't have any idea what was going on but a love for the written word was instilled. Thank you as well for your daily phone calls asking me how the book is going, what the latest email from my editor said and whether we'd sorted out a title yet or not. Your support has been a constant throughout my whole life and for that I am so very grateful (you old fart).

To my gorgeous girls – Billie and Bo – it's no exaggeration when I say that you have taught me more than I could ever hope to teach you. There were times when the only place I could imagine a better version of myself was in your faces when you looked at me with unconditional love in your eyes. You are by far the biggest influences on my life and I will spend the rest of my life trying to be the mama you deserve.

Finally, to my husband Jimmy. It's hard to know where to start. We've seen some shit through the years, but somehow we made it out the other side. I hope you see this book as I do – a testament to all the hard work we've both done, the hours and hours of couples' therapy (thank you to our incredible therapist . . . if you can fix us, you can fix anyone), the leaps of faith we both took when it came to being honest and vulnerable, the willingness to focus on our own part in things and to give up our feral need to prove that it was the other's fault. You led the way and I *eventually* followed. You really are the only human I want to do life with.

If I have missed anyone, please know it is in no way a reflection on you or on everything you've done for me. It's, quite simply, because I am perimenopausal, under pressure to get this over to the publisher and plagued by chronic forgetfulness. Please accept my apologies!

About the Author

Cat Sims is an author, podcaster and content creator still trying to figure out the whole 'adulting' thing. She has built a loyal following by documenting the beautifully chaotic reality of being a midlife woman, wife and mother – saying the things the rest of us are too afraid to admit. She is also the founder of Not So Smug Now, an online platform dedicated to making women feel seen and to proving that no matter how shitty they feel about things, they are never the only one. Her podcast, *You're Never The Only One*, runs alongside her popular Substack feed.